Praise for Jam

'White River is a passionate and astute piece of work. A journey-book in the tradition of Basho's Narrow Road to a Far Province, mixing poetry, prose and meditation, White River follows the Findhorn from its sea-mouth to its source up in the Monadhliaths. Jamie Whittle is never blind to modernity's grip on the river, but never deaf to the river's old magic either.'

Robert Macfarlane
Author of Mountains of the Mind,
The Wild Places and The Old Ways

'This is a book that should be read by every student of the land, all those who work on the land, and everyone who finds renewal and recreation on it.'

Cameron McNeish
editor of TGO and author of
The Wilderness World of Cameron McNeish
and The Sutherland Trail

'Jamie Whittle's book is based on two journeys, the first a tramp upstream from the white sands of Culbin to the mist-shrouded puddles high in the Monadhliaths where the infant Findhorn is daily reborn. The second is Jamie's return by canoe. The highly original result is an account of both the river itself and of his thoughts on man's place within the natural world of today. Take it from me, this is an important book and Jamie Whittle is a wonderful writer.'

Dr Richard Shelton
Research Director, Atlantic Salmon Trust
and author of To Sea and Back

'There's no need to have heard of the Findhorn or know where it is to enjoy this very readable book. For anyone who loves wild nature and is concerned about what is happening White River is highly recommended.'

Chris Townsend
Author of Grizzly Bears and Razor Clams,
A Year in the Life of the Cairngorms,
The Backpackers Handbook, and Crossing Arizona

'White River is one of those rare environmental books that, more than a local travelogue, takes us on a journey to the soul of modern times. Whittle holds the lawyer's scales of balance as he goes. He sees that the River Findhorn meanders between two banks and that one is busy with economics and practical matters, while the raises the eye to beauty and its ideals. We need both of these banks or else we come undone. But if we can walk as Whittle so elegantly and eloquently does – constantly shifting equilibrium from bank to bank – we can glide through this potential paradise that is our Earth.'

Alastair McIntosh

Jamie Whittle is an environmental lawyer and ski instructor who grew up beside the River Findhorn near Forres in the north of Scotland. He was a Morehead Scholar to the University of North Carolina at Chapel Hill, USA, where he earned a BA in Modern Languages with Honours, before returning to Scotland to study Law at the University of Edinburgh, and completing an MSc with Distinction in Human Ecology at the Centre for Human Ecology. Passionate about the outdoors, he has travelled extensively and enjoys exploring the wilder corners of the Scottish Highlands and Islands. He lives with his family near Hopeman on the Moray Coast.

WHITE RIVER

A Journey up and down the River Findhorn

Jamie Whittle

SANDSTONE**PRESS**
HIGHLAND | SCOTLAND

First published 2007 in Great Britain by
Sandstone Press Ltd
PO Box 5725,
1 High Street,
Dingwall,
Ross-shire,
IV15 9WJ,
Scotland

This edition published by Sandstone Press 2013
Copyright © Jamie Whittle 2007

Editor: Robert Davidson

ISBN: 978-1-908737-23-6
ISBNe: 978-1-908737-24-3

All royalties from White River go towards conservation
work in the River Findhorn watershed

WARNING AND DISCLAIMER

Whilst canoeing and kayaking can be good for your health, paddling on rivers
such as the River Findhorn can be hazardous. The descriptions of sections
of the river and various rapids should NOT be relied upon as an accurate
guide – rivers change their composition frequently and the River Findhorn
is susceptible to flash flooding. The author and publisher accept no liability
whatsoever for any reliance placed on White River as a guide to paddling or
walking the River Findhorn.

Typeset by Iolaire Typesetting. Newtonmore
Cover by River Design, Edinburgh
Printed and bound by TOTEM, Poland

For Tarka, whitewater terrier.

Contents

Acknowledgements

There are many people I wish to thank for their help, inspiration and encouragement with this project – and in the wider sense, too, for teaching me about mountains, rivers and creativity – and these include in particular: Alastair McIntosh, Sam Graham, John Talbot, Drennan Watson, Ulrich Loening and the staff and students at the Centre for Human Ecology; Matthew Stilwell; Megan Mazzocchi and the Morehead Programme; Helena Norberg Hodge, Eric Higbee, Sam Harrison, and the Ladakh Project; Roy Dennis; Dr Dick Shelton; Steve MacDonald and Anna Gordon; Jim Miller, Mike Farris, Richard Dugas, Rob Wood and the instructors and students on the COLT programme at Strathcona Park Lodge; Christian and Jackie Mark; Andy and Gill Spink, Colin and Karen Johnson and the Tiree surf posse; the late Hugh McBean; Ian Gordon; the late George Ritchie; Jeanette Duff; the Gordon Cumming family; James Stuart; Tony and Ali Brown; Clodagh Norriss; Sophie Ingleby; Neil and Claire Birnie; Mags Mackean; Dave Key; James Hawkins; Alasdair and Panny Laing; Coulmony Estate; the late Lord Balgonie; Cawdor Estate; the late Mary Rose; Lewis Rose; Dave and Fiona Thomson; Sandy and Sophie Dey; Coignafearn Estate; the late Professor Robert Kirkpatrick; Louise Mackenzie; Fiona Hill; Moira and James Ingleby; Jo Darling; Robert Davidson and Moira Forsyth at Sandstone Press; Great Granny Griz; my Mum and Dad for all their support; and Samara not least for being so patient about the never ending final draft.

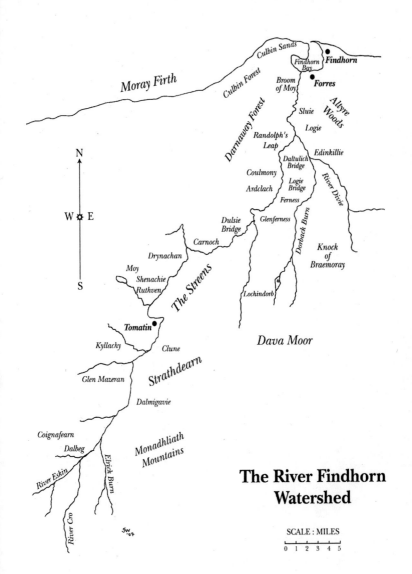

The River Findhorn
Watershed

SCALE : MILES

0 1 2 3 4 5

Introduction

I first saw the River Findhorn when I was three years old. At the time my family was living in the village of Findhorn at the mouth of the river. It was one of those unforgettable summer days in Scotland when it is almost too hot to be on the coast, and so my parents and some of their friends decided to take their children swimming upriver. Turning off the main road, we bumped along the potholes and tree roots of an overgrown forestry track as broom and rhododendron branches sprang through the open windows of the car. Clambering out barefoot onto the thick grass and mud, a strange noise – denser than the wind but softer than the crash of a wave – hummed through the cool air that hovered beneath the pines. Shivering in the darkness of the trees I tiptoed along the needles carpeting the path, and moved towards the source of this mysterious sound. At the far side of the wood I set eyes upon a sight that has both haunted and captivated me ever since: a giant river the colour of black tea, surrounded by cliffs stretching up to the clouds, with islands of sand and trees and peninsulas of stone.

The river rises in the Monadhliath Mountains, which lie between the Cairngorms and the Great Glen, and then flows for around seventy miles in a north-easterly direction towards the Moray Firth. From the remoteness of the mountains, the

Findhorn then works its way through the valley of Strathdearn and across the northern edge of the Dava Moor, before entering a lengthy gorge section that cuts through the forests down to the coastal plain. Unlike the neighbouring River Spey, which passes through a number of towns, the Findhorn only passes two settlements – Tomatin and Forres – before emptying at the sea beside the village of Findhorn. Most of the ground adjacent to the river is owned by a series of private estates, and there is a wide range of land use. The Findhorn is notorious for its flash floods – or spates – following rain on the high ground, when the river barrels down in a bore. This unpredictability combined with the abundance of whitewater (some rapids are categorised as grade 5) means that the Findhorn is not a river to be taken lightly.

It was in the summer of 2000 that the idea of exploring and writing about the River Findhorn first emerged. I was part way through my Masters degree in Human Ecology at the Centre for Human Ecology. An element of the course had been studying the connections between people and the places in which they dwell. From the course reading list, three books were especially inspiring: Henry Thoreau's Walden, Aldo Leopold's A Sand County Almanac and Gary Snyder's A Place in Space. Each writer demonstrated such profound awareness of his natural surroundings, and was able to convey the subtleties and rhythms of the land. I was also introduced to the work of Kenneth White, and shall never forget listening to a recording of his poem 'Labrador' for the first time, and being awoken by the sense of movement and discovery that is possible in the world.

Then came the term paper for the course. The topic was to write about your relationship with a particular element of the natural world. Ever since my family had moved upriver to the

INTRODUCTION

Altyre Woods when I was four, the River Findhorn had been a constant in my life, always drawing me back from wherever I was with its magnetic pull. The first draft of the term paper was filled with a series of anecdotes about the River Findhorn. The difficulty I faced was that I just didn't know how to penetrate this level and write more directly about the river. My first few efforts at describing the river were embarrassing. I felt awkward. The writing was blocked. There was no flow. I couldn't figure out how to write about a river. I also realised that I didn't really know the river. The easiest solution seemed to be to write the term paper on something completely different and less personal. My tutor's short response to my plea was that I needed to discover the river's poetry.

Ideas began to melt. The term paper proved to be the seed of my dissertation, which was a study of the human ecology along the River Findhorn. Human ecology – broadly – is the interface between ecology and society, and how each affect and define the other. To study the river would require journeying its length, and the blend of walking upstream and then paddling the river back down by canoe seemed the most complete approach. The only problem was that I had done very little whitewater canoeing at the time. Although I had been on an Outward Bound expedition in America some years previously when I had the chance to paddle through the wilderness of the Boundary Waters in Minnesota, most of the canoeing had been on flat water. So I bought a canoe, went on a whitewater safety course, and began paddling short sections of the river to build up my experience.

The journey upriver began in late May 2001. The country was just coming to the end of the foot and mouth epidemic, which had ruined the livelihoods of thousands of farmers. Access to the countryside was a major issue, and as a result it seemed best to check with proprietors along the river whether they would be okay with me walking across their land. In most cases, estates were very cooperative and suggested a preferred route.

I estimated that it would take about five days from the Culbin Sands on the coast to the heart of the Monadhliath Mountains, and loaded up my pack with enough food to last. As well as food, I packed a tent, a light sleeping bag, sleeping mat, stove and cooking gear, spare clothes, waterproofs, first aid and blister kit, odds and ends kit (knife, lighters, duck tape, compass, head torch and batteries), a series of Ordnance Survey maps, a copy of Dogen's Scripture on Mountains and Waters and a notebook.

Given both the logistics and my relative inexperience of whitewater canoeing, I decided to separate the upstream and downstream elements, and to embark on the canoe journey at some point in June. For the downstream section I paddled a Mad River 'Teton' – a 16-foot-long canoe made of polyethylene. The 'Teton' is a sturdy boat for the likes of the Findhorn where you are likely to hit rocks. However, it is a heavy boat and you certainly feel its weight when it comes to portaging the canoe around unnavigable stretches of water. In order to travel more lightly on the river and so make navigation far easier, I opted to paddle the river in five separate sections, returning home at the end of each day instead of carrying extra gear and camping out. Although it would be possible to start higher up the river on the back of a spate, I chose to begin the paddling section at Tomatin. I also opted to skip the section between Randolph's Leap and Sluie, given that this is a highly technical stretch of water, and one more suited for a kayak rather than the canoe I was paddling.

Throughout the journey I took notes. Back at my desk I

then integrated these field notes with research on a variety of disciplines such as ecology, history, psychology, mythology, philosophy, economics and law. When you start studying a river, you begin to see that it is connected to everything on the planet, and this limitlessness created a challenge with research in deciding where to draw the line. On a physical level, river water is connected to the seas and oceans, to clouds and rain and snow. A river is tipped downwards by mountains, fringed by forests and farmland, and welcomed by the coast. The water and surrounding land are inhabited by a diversity of species, some of which migrate to distant parts of the world in certain periods of the year, and some of which spend their entire lives in and around the river environment. So too with the people that come to the river – some remain for their lifetimes, some migrate for periods of the year, and some visit for only a short while. The whole is a complex, boundless space that never reaches an ultimate definition or end point.

In order to synthesise these different fields of study and try to articulate the rhythm of the river and its many elements, I tried to write in an 'ecological' style – mixing poetry with prose, and grounded observation with short essays on a variety of environmental and cultural issues. This approach seemed the only way I could run these necessary components into one.

Six 'upstream' chapters culminating in the section in the Monadhliaths were submitted as my Masters dissertation. Once the degree was over, however, the project felt incomplete. There was the downstream section to write about. Also, many questions that had arisen during the study remained unanswered in my mind – or at least, my understanding of a number of issues was untested. So began a process of extending the original dissertation into a book.

WHITE RIVER

Six years on since the journey into the mountains and back to the sea, the book is now finally complete. When I first considered writing a short paper about the River Findhorn, I had no idea where the project would lead. Never did I imagine when making the journey that I would write a book. I had no idea at that time that I would become so enraptured with canoeing that I would travel to British Columbia a few years later to train as an outdoors instructor. During the process of exploring the watershed and discovering the river in greater depth, I had no notion that this connection would so affirm my commitment to the work I now do as an environmental lawyer.

The journey brought me to wild places along the river that are achingly beautiful. Conversely, I also witnessed places where the land has been abused and where there is need of restoration. I have been struck by the range of people for whom the River Findhorn is important – be it for recreation, its economic provision, its wildlife, its sanctuary. That enthusiasm gives me genuine hope in these changing times, when the environment is under greater pressure from human impacts than ever before. Humanity faces the most fascinating – yet serious – challenge it has ever had to address collectively, and it is one that demands creativity, care and commitment. In seeking direction, we can turn to the teachings of the natural world. By connecting with the rhythms of the land, our decisions about what is appropriate become all the wiser.

Half Davoch, Forres
December 2007

WHITE RIVER

A Journey up and down the River Findhorn

CHAPTER ONE

The White Shore

'You did not come into this world. You came out of it,
like a wave from the ocean. You are not a stranger here.'
Alan Watts, 'On the Tantra'[1]

The tide is out. Waves somersault onto the shore, their carbonated frenzy lunging up the beach. In the wake of the surf, the clear, shallow water reveals intricate patterns of seaweed and sand. Within seconds each creation vanishes forever, erased by a wave slipping back out to sea.

A gannet spies its breakfast from an old netting post. The keel of an abandoned Zulu boat lies half-buried in the sand, like the spine and ribs of a whale carcass. The trunk of a giant pine has become lodged on the beach – its cracks and pockets are the thrones of pebbles.

Standing on the Culbin Sands there is a sense of immense space. In a sweep from Ben Wyvis in the west, over the Soutars and the gaping mouth of the Cromarty Firth, to Morvern and the north lands of Sutherland and Caithness melting into the horizon, the eye is drawn seawards to the vastness of an open sky. No land lies between this white shore and the Scandinavian coast, only sea.

There is tonic in this wind-battered, wave-pummelled coast. A healthy madness where the gulls whirl.

WHITE RIVER

At the edge of the interior, I think of those travellers who would have arrived here in ancient times. The relief of a shore. The apprehension of what lies beyond. The anticipation of exploration.

> Out East
> Over the sea,
> The sky is blackening

Moving across the corrugations of sand, I make for the Scots pines at the top of the dunes to shelter from a probable soaking in the next ten minutes. Every step up the dune triggers a mini avalanche of sand. The rim of the dune is matted with marram grass and pine needles. I drop my pack beneath one of the larger trees and pull on waterproofs. With a cup of tea from my Thermos, I settle down to watch this morning's storm funnel its way up the Firth.

It's going to take four to five days to walk the length of the River Findhorn from the coast to the mountains. I could have dropped into the source from the back of Newtonmore in upper Speyside and walked downstream. Instead I've chosen to walk upstream and canoe back down which feels more natural and complete. There will be sections, too, where what paths that exist along the river run out, or take detours away from the river bank. The return journey by canoe will allow me to gain as full a sense of the river as possible.

It's strange – for the past week I've had trouble sleeping at night, having awaited the start of this journey for over a year now. It's not the weather or the natural environment that concerns me. It's people. It's the meetings along the way that I'm most nervous about. Will folk be hostile or welcoming? Humans are an unpredictable species.

THE WHITE SHORE

Weather, on the other hand, seems far easier to predict as I watch the front move in from my outlook beneath the pines. First comes the calm, followed by the sermon of thunder, and then the chorus of rain.

Gulls signal the end of this three-part movement by taking to the air in the storm's wake. The last drops of rain now fallen, I remove my waterproofs, shoulder the pack and slip down the dune back to the beach. The journey is now underway.

The last few hundred yards of the River Findhorn divide the Culbin Sands from the beach at Findhorn. Already mixed with the outgoing salt water from Findhorn Bay, the river races over barnacled channels to the firth where clapotis waves rise in the fracas of colliding currents. Lipping around the entrance to the bay is a sandbank spit where common seals lounge.[2] It is difficult to count their exact number – fifty, perhaps sixty. Waiting for the tide to turn and the bay to fill with salmon running upriver, the seals keep watch on human presence. Anyone approaching the spit on foot or by sea-kayak is sure to trigger an evacuation of the seal colony off the sand and into the water. Despite this wariness, you invariably find seals trailing your kayak. Yet turn quickly for a glimpse and the seal will have plunged leaving only bubbles.

In maritime folklore seals are considered not only the equals of humans, but are thought to have royal blood.[3] As the story goes, the children of one of the kings of Norway were put under a spell by their wicked stepmother who (jealous of the children's natural good looks) turned them into seals. Three times a year on the full moon, it is said, they reappear in human form, so stunningly beautiful that humans are rendered powerless and cannot help but fall in love with them.

Throughout the northern and western reaches of Scotland – the Hebrides, Orkney and Shetland – are families who similarly have claimed descent from seals. These 'seal-folk' (as they are referred to in the Hebrides) or 'Finn-folk' (Orkney and Shetland) are thought to be related to the Sjo-Sami (or coastal Lapps) of Northern Norway. Tales of a sea-faring people called the 'Finn-folk' who travelled by kayak in the 17th century from Scandinavia to Orkney may substantiate this link.[4] Some of the more notable characteristics of these seal-folk include being able to survive in the most extreme Atlantic conditions as well as having the ability to paddle a sea-kayak with the utmost skill.

Going back further in time, in the mid-19th century Captain Frederick W.L. Thomas wrote of a people who moved throughout the coastal regions of the far north:[5]

> ... the close of the ice period is not so far distant. Whenever it occurred, colonies of men would no doubt follow up the coast in the same manner in which the Esquimaux have distributed themselves in the Arctic regions. As the climate ameliorated, vegetation would increase, and a littoral mode of life – apparently the most primitive of all – would be mixed up with and partly superseded by a pastoral one ... Now the primitive people of our island and of the whole of Europe were most probably of Turanian division, and all represented in Europe by the Lapps and Finns ... My own opinion is that this race held possession for thousands of years.

In the same vein, the ethnologist Claude Levi-Strauss wrote of a sub-Arctic culture[6] stretching from Canada across to Scandinavia and Siberia, which kept close contact throughout this northern region. Levi-Strauss suggested that the Celts may well have borrowed myths from this sub-Arctic culture, which might explain how the Holy Grail cycle is more similar to the legends of Native American Indians than European myths.

Could it be that Northern Scotland formed part of a sub-Arctic, 'seal-folk', Lapp/Finn culture? And if the Finns were early visitors to this white shore, does that provide the reason why the bay and river were named Fin-dhorn?

When we look at the bigger – and longer – picture of this possible sub-Arctic, 'Hyperborean'[7] culture, we may in fact find ourselves connected to a cultural and geographical expanse not yet acknowledged by modern society. But so what? Why should we look northwards?

I would submit that modern Scotland – indeed modern Europe – lacks substantial cultural identity. By this I don't mean a lack of music or art or literature. What is lacking, rather, is an understanding of who we are and a connection to where we live.

This erosion of cultural identity began in the 17th century with the rationalist, reductionist philosophies of the likes of Descartes, Newton and Bacon during the Enlightenment. Emphasising a mechanistic worldview, a split between mind and matter, and a separation between humans and the natural world, these theories primed the Scientific Revolution and helped shape the economic systems and industrial practices that form the foundations upon which the modern world operates.

The economies of European countries have grown beyond all recognition, and for that reason many would say that we are far better off in the modern world than those living 300 years ago. Yet when it comes to accounting for this growth, we start to see that it is not without its costs. These 'enlightened' theories mistook natural capital for natural income and as a result the modern world has based much of its growth on finite resources.

Increasingly, as natural resources have become exhausted and wider markets with cheaper goods from abroad have challenged domestic production, employment has become more transient, drawing labour away both from the rural hinterland towards urban centres as well as from city to city. One of the penalties of this transience is that community cohesion tends to wither. Over a period of time, therefore, the economic systems we currently have in place have dislocated people from place. Once caught up in this current, it becomes difficult to retain a point of contact with the natural world and see where modern society is heading.

Frederick Nietzsche was one of a number of thinkers to point out this movement when he wrote in the preface to The Will to Power:[8]

> For some time now, our whole European culture has been moving as toward a catastrophe, with a tortured tension that is growing from decade to decade: restlessly, violently, headlong, like a river that wants to reach the end, that no longer reflects, which is afraid to reflect.

We now stand at a crossroads of danger and opportunity. We live in a time when the climate is changing as an undeniable result of carbon dioxide emitted from human activity, when international politics is a nerve-shaken junkie in search of oil and paranoid of strangers, when species face extinction across every environmental zone on the planet, when wilderness is cashed in at the bank by men in hard hats, and when communities (fragile as alpine plants) face the sentence of homogenisation.

If we continue down this path much further, we shall pass a point of no return from which the damage we have done to the planet cannot be undone.

It's time for new movement.

When we are reminded about this catalogue of modern dysfunction in the news and see it in varying dimensions in our own lives, there are often two natural reactions we can adopt: to feel an overwhelming sense of powerlessness and/or to numb ourselves to reality by burying our heads in the sand. Having experienced both options myself, my own view is that they lead to stagnation.

A large part of the problem comes from feeling lost. As the French painter Paul Gauguin asked in his Tahitian masterpiece painted in 1897: 'Where Do We Come From? What Are We? Where Are We Going?'.[9] It is these fundamental questions that form the first steps of an exploration of our place in the world. Without a grounded understanding of where we have come from, the present remains out of context.

In the past, cultures remained in touch with their roots through a tradition of story-telling. In the race to modernise Northern Scotland (and much of the rest of the world) over the past three centuries or so, slowly and stealthily this exchange of information, countless generations old, has been washed away. Roots create grounding, and with grounding there is stability. Roots form the reference point we need in order to develop cultural expression, anchoring us to the wisdom of the past yet at the same time providing a contemporary freedom in which to move.

Walking along the west shore of the bay, where the oyster catchers rise together and sweep across the breeze, I think about the purpose of this journey. From sea to source and back again, this journey up and down the River Findhorn is about trying to rediscover a reference point – culturally and ecologically – and moving beyond accustomed bounds into a new space. Just

9

what will be seen and learned in this new space is unknown, but a greater understanding of the watershed may allow a more accurate articulation of the world. As the conservationist John Muir once wrote, 'When we try to pick out anything by itself, we find it hitched to everything else in the universe.'[10] Linked to mountains, forests, species and peoples, weather patterns, coasts and oceans, a river is essentially linked to everything on the planet. From studying the local, there is both a parallel and a correspondence with the global.

There is also the physical experience of walking with a full pack up into the mountains, and then paddling the river back down to the sea. I'm looking forward to the challenge of travelling through varying terrains in different weathers. There is a psychological element, too, of travelling solo and becoming comfortable with my own company and timeframe. All of this to be experienced in the local area, literally opening the door and setting off.

It's ironic that I've travelled to a number of faraway countries, but up until now have never travelled on foot or by canoe the entire length of the river along which I live. Maybe I've just had my priorities wrong, or have foolishly believed that to understand the world it has been necessary to travel abroad. I used to hold fast to the idea that the only way to see the world was via a long-haul flight, and it is, certainly, one way to see the world – patching images together to form a pattern of reality. Now I believe that to see the world you can also remain in one place. Like the Sanskrit prayer that says, 'Look to this day for it is life, the very life of life/ In its brief course lie all the realities and truths of existence.'

The key is to pay attention and to learn to read the signs. The signs help guide us, drawing our attention to the dangers and opportunities along the way, deepening our consciousness of where we are and increasing our awareness of a place. Recognising a sign requires an understanding of language – the language of place. To an extent it means knowing the human languages of a place, such as the influence of Gaelic upstream in the mountains. But the real language of place is poetry. It is song. As Bruce Chatwin described in The Songlines[11] a song was essentially your means of navigating your way across the land. The song was passed down from generation to generation and described the world as the ancestors experienced it. By going 'walkabout', an Aboriginal would make a journey in the footsteps of his ancestors. In experiencing the world in this manner, someone on Walkabout would know what state the land should be and therefore how it could be protected.

I've never been taught the songlines of the River Findhorn. Nevertheless I like to think of this journey as going walkabout. Without having learned the song from others, however, the task begins of reading the land anew and 'singing it into existence'. It means trying to release conditioned thoughts about a place and engaging in a contact with the natural world that is direct and which avoids premeditation.

Songs of the river must have existed at one time: songs about the best locations for gathering and hunting, songs about how to travel from one place to the next. For thousands of years people would have travelled the length of the river into the hinterlands in spring, returning in dugout canoes and skin-covered coracles to the coast in late autumn[12]

> Upstream
> When the spring salmon run
> And the geese fly North
> To the Arctic

11

If a songline needs a rhythm section then let's start with geese and salmon. Both species have impeccable timing.

> The salmon
> In its silver suit
> Tailored
> Beneath icebergs
>
> The syncopated
> Slipstream
> Of geese
> Calling out
> A quick march
> Across the silver light

The Picts, it would seem, were in step with this rhythm. A stone carving discovered at Easterton of Roseisle, (which lies between Findhorn Bay and the site of the Pictish fort at Burghead) displays a goose above a salmon[13] Two species that indicate – like clockwork – the times of the year. It is quite possible that these Pictish symbols originated from the relationship between the shaman of each Pictish tribe and the tribes' various animal totems. A shaman was required, amongst other tasks, to find the best hunting grounds as well as to pacify the spirits of animals[14] Describing the shaman's methods, Elizabeth Sutherland comments in her study In Search of the Picts[15]

The spirit of the shaman was able in trance-state and after long periods of endurance to enter the dangerous Otherworld of the spirits. For safety he would wear the hide of the creature he hoped to placate. There were many earthly doors to this world, such as caves, burial cairns and springs, through which he could enter

... These Otherworld visits made it possible for the shaman to become close to a certain spirit whom he trusted to show favour to his tribe. In return the group adopted the creature as its totem and took its name. It was then taboo to hunt that creature except at festivals sacred to its person ... As a result of his contact with the spirit world the shaman was to become diviner, healer and law-giver to the tribe.

Yet it was not simply a case of the shaman ensuring that the tribe found sufficient food and resources from the land. It was also the shaman's job to make sure that reciprocal nourishment was given back to the land by humans. Through this connection to the land and awareness of its capacity and limits, an ancient practice of sustainable living was achieved.[16]

Given that the Picts, it is believed, hailed from Scythia[17] and the fact that writers such as Herodotus documented a shamanic tradition as being central to Scythian culture, it is quite possible that any Pictish shamanic tradition found its roots in Central Asia.[18] Add to this a sub-Arctic culture also rooted in shamanism – Lapp, Inuit (Eskimo), Siberian – and the fabric of an original cultural identity grows ever richer and deeper. Sheriff Rampini of Nairn made reference to the 'demon-like Druids' of the Picts, in his History of Moray and Nairn.[19] Kenneth White suggested a portrait of these Pictish shamans being more akin to the medicine-men of the American Indians or the angekok of the Eskimo and dressed in skins, rather than the picture we often attribute to druids being dressed in white togas and cutting mistletoe with sickles.[20]

Moray was a hub in the 'mythical heartland' of the Picts.[21] It remained this way for a number of reasons including the fact that the Picts managed to prevent the Romans from entering the Highlands. Indeed the Emperor Septimius Severus' plan to punish the Pictish and Caledonian tribes because of their repeated antagonism of the Roman army was a tactic that went badly wrong for his forces. Severus' campaign against 'the painted people' resulted in the loss of 50,000 Roman soldiers and a long walk home to Italy. The Pictish warriors, as it is chronicled, were not only physically tough but were also highly advanced in the arts of war.[22]

Another reason for the long-lived legacy of the Picts in the area was the fact that when the Gaels began to move into the region from the West coast and from Ireland, rather than there being a great invasion, there began a 'long process of cultural assimilation'[23] albeit accelerated by the Viking raids taking place in the West which pushed the Gaels over into Pictland.

This isn't to say that the Vikings didn't land their 'dragon-ships' upon this white shore. On the contrary, Scandinavian invasions and settlement dominated the 8th, 9th and 10th Centuries.[24] Of the two distinct nations that formed the Vikings – the fair-haired Finngaill of Norway and the dark-haired Dubhgaill of Denmark – it was the Finngaill that came to colonise Moray. Both the events and names of the characters that form the history of these Viking years are colourful, and the following is a mere flavour of what took place.

Thorstein the Red was the first to conquer Moray, followed by Sigurd, the first Jarl of Orkney and Caithness. After murdering Maelbrigd the Buck-Tooth (the Maormar or clan chief of Moray), Sigurd then scratched his leg against Maelbrigd's famous tooth only to die a few days later. Maelbrigd's successors, Finleikr and Finlay, were defeated in battle by another Sigurd (Sigurd the Stout) whose secret weapon was 'a magic banner bearing the

14

device of an ink-black raven soaring on the wings of the wind' – a gift from his sorceress mother.

King Malcolm MacKenneth of Scotland (1005–1034) decided to marry off one of his daughters to Sigurd the Stout, as well as conferring upon him the earldom of Caithness. Malcolm's other daughter, Beatrice, married Crinan, the abbot of Dunkeld, and named their son Duncan.

When Duncan later became king he soon locked horns with his arch-rival and cousin, the mightily named Thorfinn (son of Sigurd the Stout), Jarl of Orkney and Shetland and Earl of Caithness and Sutherland. On 14 August 1040, the armies of Duncan and Thorfinn met for battle at Burghead. Thorfinn won the battle, aided by the Maormar of Moray, a certain Macbeth, who is said to have slain Duncan after the battle while he was resting at Pitgaveny.[25]

The area is just so rich in human history.

Across the bay, the brightly washed houses of the village of Findhorn sit nestled into the shore. At one time Findhorn formed a bustling trading port with ships entering the bay laden with goods from afar and exiting with resources from the interior. There also used to be a fishing fleet, but no more.

> The beach
> Is strewn
> With mussel shells
> Of lapis blue
> And ivory
>
> Combs
> Cockles, spirals

WHITE RIVER

Scots pine bark
Fish nets
And gull feathers

Stones
Rounded by the rapids
Upriver
Then polished
By the waves
To a varnish

Red shanks
Curlew
And oyster catchers
Stalk
The slack water

A sparrowhawk
Cracks
The air
Accelerating
The coastal tempo

I start thinking more about the river's name: Findhorn – White River. It seems paradoxical given its dark and peaty waters. But the general feeling amongst those who have written about the River Findhorn is that the white (fionn in Gaelic) refers to the 'shimmering sands' of the shore. This theory is plausible when you consider that until the early part of the last century the Culbin Forest (as we now know it) did not exist, but instead formed the largest desert in Northern Europe. The pines that now fortify the dunes were planted to prevent the sandstorms that buried farms and villages, particularly during the late 17th century with the Great Sand Drift occurring in 1694. Pioneers of the afforestation of the Culbin featured Grant of Kincorth who planted marram grass to stabilise the sand in 1839. The major breakthrough, however, came with John Grigor, a tree nurseryman from Forres, who in 1841 planted pines using a thatching technique of planting seedlings amidst branches and tops of trees that were placed across the sand.

1922 saw the Forestry Commission begin to manage the area, planting Scots and Corsican Pines, as well as varieties of Lodgepole pine, Douglas fir and Norway spruce, again using John Grigor's thatching technique where necessary[26] Today a mature forest is managed for timber production, as well as providing habitats for fauna and flora and a maze of roads and footpaths for walkers, riders and cyclists. The Culbin represents, therefore, an excellent example of humans working with nature to create an economic resource, environmental services, wildlife habitats and recreational amenity. There can be no greater symbol of hope than a tree taking root in a desert.

If we accept the reason for the White River being named as such because of the sands around the bay, however, are we not limiting all thought merely to the end of the river? Do we not indeed fall into the trap Nietzsche warned about of rushing straight to the end and being afraid to reflect? There's at least 70 miles between here and the source of the River Findhorn – that's 70 or so miles of space and possibility to look for clues. Let's not forget that although the name Findhorn is generally attributed to the Gaelic words of fionn (white) and eren (a stream that forms the boundary between two districts)[27] the Gaels are thought to have moved down river from West to East. So the

Gaels may well have named the river for reasons based around their observations upstream. As Thomas Henderson described in[28]

> Down this valley of Strathdearn [the upper Findhorn], 'Ireland's Strath', came the invading Gaels from Ireland and settled in such numbers as to impose their system of names on plain and hill and stream ... The old name of the valley from the source to Tomatin was 'The Threshold of the Gaels', so, difficult as the passages from the Great Glen and Strathspey are, we may perhaps conclude that Strathdearn was one of the roads by which the Irish Celts made their way to the plains of the East to settle among the mysterious Picts.

Even though Henderson himself thought that the river meant 'The White Ireland', attributing this name to the sands in the estuary, there is another idea we should at this point consider. The idea I'm suggesting is the 'white world' – a philosophical-poetic concept that appears amongst a host of writers and thinkers from Hermann Melville to D.H. Lawrence, from Frederick Nietzsche to Robinson Jeffers, in the poetry of the Chinese Taoists and the Zen masters, and which has been articulated most coherently in recent times by Kenneth White.

The 'white world' is an elemental place – but equally a state of mind – of intense, almost blinding clarity, where awareness and groundedness cut through the fuzz and confusion of modernity, to witness a truth and reality in the naked light of the natural world.

Maybe, just maybe, the early settlers to the area named the White River as such for this very sense. Perhaps there lies an elemental sense up and down the River Findhorn that conjures an intense energy to this fundamental, deep-rooted level of perception and existence. Maybe the White River was a springboard into this white world, and remains so today. All we need is the map to guide us along this path of experience. That map is the song.

Rounding the bay to Elvin Point the rain returns, this time from a more northerly direction than the thunderstorm nearly an hour ago. I make for the edge of the Culbin Forest and rest for a while beneath a Scots pine. Looking out towards the point at Binsness in the direction of Forres, I watch an osprey fishing for flatfish beyond the river mouth where the salt water starts. Twice it tries to move into strike position, but each time the gulls cause a diversion breaking its concentration and poise. Strike three and the osprey hovers almost like a kestrel some 40 feet above sea level, then tucks, plummets, checks a few feet from the water, plunges then surfaces, before heading back upriver for a family lunch of flounder.

Ospreys are a wildlife-reintroduction success story. Although rare sightings of the birds in the area during the late 19th and early to mid-20th centuries have been recorded, the osprey has returned from the brink of extinction in Scotland over the past 50 years. Returning to Scotland in the late 1950s, a pair built a nest at Loch Garten in Upper Speyside in 1966, and then raised two young in the following year[29] The navigational skills of ospreys are beyond category, being able to return to the same nest each year all the way from Africa, and arriving within the same small time window in late March and early April. Ospreys are able to navigate locally from visual memory, but when it comes to transcontinental crossings they use another method. As proven in a planetarium in Germany some years ago, certain migratory species of birds have the ability to navigate celestially.

Therefore, it is thought that osprey chicks are born with a map of the night sky genetically imprinted in their brains[30] Before the availability of GPS navigation, sailors and explorers similarly tracked their way across the Earth's wild expanses using the stars as their reference points. There is a magic and beauty in such an astronomical connection – that we, like birds, can find our way through the wilds if we develop the capacity to read what surrounds us in the natural world.

Again, the recovery of ospreys is testimony to what can be achieved in the natural world when humans determine to protect and restore wildlife, and to lend a helping hand when necessary. Fortunately, the area around Findhorn Bay is afforded the very highest environmental protection – being a Special Protection Area for birds under the European Birds Directive, a Ramsar site in terms of the International Treaty for the Protection of Wetland Birds (Ramsar being located in the marshlands of southern Iran), and a Special Area of Conservation in terms of the European Habitats Directive for the bottlenose dolphins and sandbanks located out in the Moray Firth. With such protected areas combined with the mandate under the Nature Conservation (Scotland) Act 2004 that all public bodies must seek to protect and promote biological diversity, we have in place a strong legal framework to enforce wildlife protection. As such it means that any proposed development in the area has to comply with the stipulations of European and national environmental law, and anyone who intentionally or recklessly disturbs, damages or destroys a protected species can face criminal sanctions.

Having laws in place for wildlife protection and restoration is essential. Equally important is an understanding by the public and both local and national government of the importance of conserving wild species and habitats, as well as a desire to carry out dynamic nature conservation initiatives. All too often when legislation trickles its way down from the European Union in Brussels to national law and policy in Scotland, the government wriggles out of applying these laws effectively. Equally, businesses that have not yet genuinely embraced sustainable development simply fail to acknowledge the importance of safeguarding the environment, and instead see economics as distinct from and superior to the natural world – the environment being given second class status at best. My point is that whilst we need laws to enforce protection of the environment, law in itself is insufficient for bringing about a necessary shift in human consciousness that will lead to the Earth being more greatly cherished and environmental catastrophe averted. Primary contact between humans and the natural world and a corresponding form of ecological education are paramount.

The bay is now beginning to fill once again with an incoming tide. Across the water spin the wind turbines at the eco-village of the Findhorn Foundation. Established in 1965, the Foundation has developed into a centre for holistic thinking and practice. Many of the buildings at the Foundation are constructed using pioneering ecological design, albeit not examples of the vernacular architecture found throughout Moray. The place draws an array of distinguished speakers to its many conferences on environmental issues, alternative medicine, comparative religion and the arts. Before my parents and I moved upriver when I was four years old, I attended the nursery school at the Foundation and so have known a good number of people that have lived there for many years. Back then it was considered somewhat taboo for locals to mix with those at the Foundation, but as sustainability has become more of a mainstream issue and people based at the Foundation have subsequently moved out into the Moray hinterland, the distinction between the radical and the traditional has lessened.

After a last glance across the water to the air force base at Kinloss, clockwise to Califer Hill, the rich farm land of the Laich of Moray at Netherton, and Nelson's Tower rising above Forres, I leave the shore and pick up one of the forest tracks through the Culbin towards Kincorth.

CHAPTER TWO

Into the Forests

'What would you in this forest of serenity? Seek you a lost self in the green shadows, or is it a home-coming in your twilight?'

Kahlil Gibran, The King Hermit[31]

There is a quiet in the Culbin Forest. The rain starts to spit its way through the pine boughs. I take the gamble of not stopping to pull on waterproofs, and argue that light rain on my clothes will compensate for the heat created by carrying a pack. Sure enough, though, within a couple of minutes the sound of the rain rattles through the forest, and I am forced to make a scramble for my jacket.

Good waterproofs are hard to find, but like all quality articles of outdoor gear are definitely worth the money. When any piece of clothing or equipment passes the test in challenging conditions, I find tremendous satisfaction. Maybe it stems back to childhood camping expeditions around Moray, the Cairngorms and the Western Isles, where getting soaked to the skin or being unable to start a fire was simply part of the learning curve. There is nothing more miserable than climbing into a wet sleeping bag having eaten a can of cold beans and a few crackers! No wonder so many people are put off outdoor living if their first experience is a damp one. When gear works, when you keep everything dry and organised, when you get a brew going in a rainstorm, and when you hunker down for the night in your tent or under the stars all warm and stomach full and weather beaten, there is freedom.

The Culbin Forest is something of a labyrinth, and being unable to see any landmarks – let alone the sun on a day of showers – it is very easy to become disoriented. I once heard of someone who was working out at the fishing station at the Old Bar between Findhorn Bay and Nairn who was lost for three days in the forest. Hopefully that won't happen to me, although I do have five days' worth of food should anything go wrong.

The tracks of sand, stone and pine needles make for speedy walking compared to the beach, and it feels good to strike a rhythm and cover ground efficiently.

By the time I reach the edge of the forest and the agricultural land at Kincorth, the rain shower has passed. Clouds slip inland across the Laich of Moray and over into Speyside. Having hoped to round the estuary on foot, given the jungle of hogweed that is rife along the banks of the lower river at this time of year, I've decided to stick to the road. I'll have the chance to explore the estuary by canoe when I return downstream. For the meanwhile I must weave my way past barley fields to join the river upstream.

> Hawthorn blossom
> And cow parsley
> Flank the road
> To Broom of Moy

Walking on a hard tarmac surface after a period of sand and then forest track feels unnatural and unforgiving. After the silence and space of the forest, it feels even stranger to have to pull into the side of the road when the occasional car or tractor passes. Because of the fast surface, the presence of traffic and the distance away from the river, there is a tendency to race. I feel a sense of wanting to be further into the journey than I already am. But as Gandhi said, 'There is more to life than increasing its speed.' Whilst it is possible to travel from Forres to Tomatin by car in 45 minutes, or by fighter jet from RAF Kinloss to the Monadhliaths in only five minutes, this journey is not about speed. It is about feeling the true distance of the river. Although there is an anticipation of wanting to be already further upriver, it's more about the journey than the destination. Every step leads me closer to the source.

Watching the roller-coaster flight line of a wood pigeon, I pause for a moment. The need to hurry subsides and I tune in to the wavelength of birdsong.

> Jackdaws and crows
> Drift
> On the wind
> Pheasants
> Snipe
> The long grass
>
> Young elms
> Groan
> In the morning breeze
> As the tattie field
> Snakes
> Its way
> Along the burn

WHITE RIVER

A blackbird
Hops
Along the roadside
Grit
Dangling a worm
In its beak

Approaching the hamlet of Broom of Moy a sign reads: 'Children at Play – 10 mph'. I'm travelling well below the speed limit. The salmon netters' bothies at Broom of Moy are still occupied, although the era of netting salmon on the River Findhorn is now past. Numbers of wild Atlantic salmon returning to rivers in Scotland have declined considerably since the 1960s and 1970s[32] and consequently many salmon netting operations were bought out with money raised by the Atlantic Salmon Conservation Trust (Scotland) in an attempt to preserve wild stocks.

During the Great Moray Floods of 1829, ten houses were completely demolished in Broom of Moy when the River Findhorn rose to such a height that only 'a few roofs peeping from the midst of the inundation' could be seen[33] A number of people drowned in this unprecedented event, as eyewitness Andrew Smith's explained:

> The water's a in aboot the hooses o' Broom o' Moy, an' some o' them hae fa'en else. Thank Providence that we hae escapit. I ken ye'll no grudge us quarters, Mr Suter. But troth I fear there's mony a ane will no hae siccan luck. There's twa families yonder wholly surrounded, and as for poor Sandy Smith! Poor Funns! Naebody can ever houp till see him or his family again.

INTO THE FORESTS

Thus the old prophecy of the river was lived out: 'Says Divie to Dorback what shall we sweep,/Through the middle o' Moy when a' men sleep.'[34]

Very different from the size and colour of its waters in August 1829 when it tore through Broom of Moy, the crow-coloured river glides lazily past the hamlet on this late spring morning. I cross the suspension bridge to the right bank of the river. The river is low today, and around 30 yards wide at this point. Forres lies across the fields, set against the backdrop of wooded hills. In the far distance to the south-west stands the mountain of the Knock of Braemoray, marking an outer edge to the forests that cover this lower part of the watershed down to the coastal plain.

I think of that contrast in Tolkien's The Lord of the Rings of moving from the safety and fruitfulness of the Shire to the mystery and challenges in the forests and mountains of Middle Earth. There's all the unpredictability of what might happen along the way. The risk that to embark on such a journey could change you forever. The possibility that friends and family might not understand your experiences. The chance that society will mock you for moving into new boundaries, uncomfortable with your new found perception and discovery of the world.

Genuine aliveness is located beyond the comfort zone, in the realm of adventure.

Matsuo Basho in The Narrow Road to the Deep North[35] described being inspired by 'the cloud-moving wind' and filled with a desire to explore the world. It is that same desire to explore that is the driving force for this journey. To immerse myself in the elements and encounter the very sap of life.

WHITE RIVER

The air is filled
With the toffee
Scent of whin

Bluebells and cowslips
Colour the undergrowth

In the pool
Below Mundole Bridge
A heron searches for fish
Moving its head and neck
Like the hypnotic dance
Of a cobra

Oyster catchers
Circle the eddies

At last, after cautiously working my way for a good half mile through a jungle of giant hogweed, I come to the edge of the forest. Bending under the first branches of beech and silver birch, I slip into the delicious coolness of the shadows and out of sight. Sunlight funnels through the foliage. Upon entering the forest, I think of the words of D.H Lawrence in his poem 'The Escape' and how time spent in forests can bring us back from the 'glass bottles of our ego' in this often anaesthetic, modern world to a sense of 'new power'.[36] There is something thirst-quenching about being in the forest and out of the wide-open space of the shore. Maybe it's because you can move more unobtrusively in the woods.

INTO THE FORESTS

But are you really
Out of sight?
The forest has eyes
Everywhere

The buzzard
Perched on an oak branch
Roe deer standing motionless
In the bracken
Red squirrels keeping watch
From the turrets of Scots pines

Nobody passes unnoticed

Some people find forests inhospitable and threatening places. Fear of ambush is one explanation why many humans (and cattle too) tend to prefer the open spaces where they can see who and what is approaching. This fear provides one of reasons why there have been centuries of fanatical deforestation throughout the world.

The term 'wilderness' once had specific reference to forests, as in the German word for a forest, Wald. Today, wilderness has come to mean many things, and there seems to be no standard yardstick or definition. Etymologically, it means 'the place of wild beasts'.[37] However, the ecologist, Aldo Leopold, once suggested that wilderness was a region that could absorb a backpacking trip two weeks' long.[38] For the explorer Robert Marshall, wilderness necessitated an area so large that it could not be traversed without mechanical means in a single day.[39] The United States Wilderness Act defines wilderness as follows:[40]

A wilderness, in contrast with those areas where man and his works dominate the landscape, is hereby recognised as an area where the earth and its community of life are untrammelled by man, where man himself is a visitor and does not remain.

For me, wilderness – in the big country sense – requires space and remoteness from human construction and industry. Being far away from help certainly tends to amplify the intensity and concentration of the experience. So too does the presence of any large animals. In deep wilderness, your keys to survival are often humility, awareness and self-reliance.

As well as the emphasis on expanse and remoteness, wilderness, as Roderick Nash points out in his seminal work Wilderness and the American Mind, can equally be defined by the feelings a place invokes. Nash suggests that a place where a person feels lost or stripped of guidance can be termed wilderness.[41]

Deserts and glaciers are the natural environments where I have felt 'stripped of guidance' most profoundly. A ski-mountaineering expedition I was part of to the North Patagonian ice cap was, I think, the most intense wilderness experience I have ever encountered. The world of seracs and crevasses, and towers of ice toppling into the sea and then rising to the surface with a deafening boom, Godzilla-like. The bad weather conditions were relentless. They say that Patagonia lures you into her web through a weather window before closing around you.

A large part of what you consider wilderness depends on where you grew up and what you are accustomed to. Having been raised in this particular forest, it is where I feel most at home in the world.

In this light, it is said that the Native American Indians could not comprehend the attitude of the European settlers who labelled North America 'a wilderness'. To the Native Americans the land was their home, with their entire cosmology revolving around the natural environment.

Wilderness in terms of what you feel from a place need not exclusively refer to the natural world. In a sense, you could argue that a city can create a wilderness experience in the psychological dimension. I'll never forget the feelings of disorientation and fear I felt during the early stages of my first post-university job, immersed in the battery acid of the corporate world. Riding that train to work in Glasgow each morning, my insides felt like an ice cavern, with any butterflies frozen solid.

It's also a question of perception. It's about learning to see.

> The history of a stone
> The trajectories of bird flight
> The line of water
> Flowing through a rapid
> The intricacies of forest grasses
> That blend of uniqueness
> And timeless maturity

Wilderness has many dimensions. The essential ingredient in each aspect of wilderness is wildness. Wildness as a quality is uncontrived and natural. Just as this dimension can be found in the natural world, so too can we find it within our own beings. When humans demonstrate this quality in their actions it is not (as might otherwise be expected) about hedonism or lost drunkenness or some drug-induced state. To me that's not really wild – more caged. An ecstasy in a non-artificially induced sense – genuine intoxication of the spirit, fully aware when every cell in your body fires with life. Fundamental to this state, therefore, is

31

an ability to live with fully integral and specifically personalised authenticity.

The poet Robert Service, most renowned for his poems set in the Yukon Klondike, summed up the imprisoned opposite of wildness in his poem, The Call of the Wild, when he wrote[42]

They have cradled you in custom, they have primed you with
    their preaching,
They have soaked you in convention through and through;
They have put you in a showcase; you're a credit to their
    teaching –
But can't you hear the Wild? – it's calling you.

Whether it's deep pine forests, remote mountain tops, whitewater or the ocean's expanse, or whether it's your own true nature (blocked up and locked away under layer upon layer of social conditioning that you need to penetrate and bring back to the surface), it is all essentially one and the same thing.

Henry Thoreau's oft-misquoted maxim, 'In Wildness is the preservation of the World', resonates true on many levels. Psychological and ecological stability are more colourful, healthier and more abundant when people, animals, plants and all living systems are free to be themselves – in their own natural order. In China, this natural order is known as li. It's so simple, yet it can be the longest journey we take in life (sometimes a journey never embarked upon by those who remain in 'the cave') to unlearn misguided human teachings and return to a point of elemental truth. Like that Zen saying of when you are born a mountain is a mountain, as you grow up it becomes analysed and perceived in contrived ways, and then upon reaching enlightenment you see it as a mountain once again. It's this progression of removing the layers until you reach a point of clarity.

One of the most perceptive descriptions of leadership I have come across was by the mountaineer, John Graham, who described good leadership as being able to liberate people so that they do what is required in the best way possible.[43] Lao Tzu wrote in a similar vein in the Tao Te Ching when he suggested that a good leader was someone who talked little, but that when his work was done and his aim fulfilled, his followers would feel as if they had accomplished the task themselves. In other words, a good leader doesn't seek to impose their ego on others and dominate the stage. Good leaders allow people to be themselves, encouraging people's natural strengths and character. Having autonomy to be yourself allows you to contribute to the whole with far greater energy and colour.

Luckily, we don't have to be perfect to be ourselves. In fact, as Joseph Campbell explained in the The Power of Myth, it's people's imperfections that make them the characters they genuinely are. Perfection is boring. Perfectionism is one of life's absolute killers.

Being yourself. Learning to be yourself. In my experience, it's that combination of facing challenging situations and then entering into reflective solitude that is the most self-educational: that cyclical 'praxis' that the Brazilian educator Paolo Freire spoke of involving action, reflection and then action again. A journey is considered by many cultures throughout time as being an archetypal way of experiencing this process.

A key ingredient in this quest for uncovering your true being and thus being able to begin living authentically comes from developing a knowledge of where you are from: learning about your domain – or becoming 'native to a place'. Every individual has their very own distinct and differentiating character, coloured by roots and environment. I certainly find that when I meet people who are themselves, unaffected by any homogenised set of social expectations, that they are far more refreshing company. They are alive.

At the root of illness and wellness lies this vital honesty, this alignment of right view, right action and right livelihood. You only need to look at yourself in the mirror to see that when things aren't right at the core, they don't manifest themselves colourfully upon the surface. It is the very same with ecology and stewardship of the land: trees simply don't grow to their fullness when placed in the wrong soil.

Nature is our academy of wildness. The lessons and role-models we need as humans to live spontaneously, released and free, are forever there in the outdoors. 'I came to the woods because I wished to live deliberately,' wrote Thoreau in Walden, 'to front only the essential facts of life, and see if I could not learn what it had to teach, and not, when I came to die, discover that I had not lived'.[44]

The right bank of the river at this section forms part of Altyre estate, owned by the Gordon Cumming family. One of the meanings of Allt in Gaelic is 'river with precipitous banks'.[45] which would seem apt given the towering sandstone cliffs that guard the river throughout this section. For centuries the Comyns (Cummings) were the most powerful clan in the area, owning the length of the right bank of the Findhorn from Logie Bridge at Glenferness all the way downstream to the plain at Forres. In the 13th century the Comyns also held the post of ranger of the Forest of Darnaway on the opposite bank of the river.[46] The name Darnaway derives from the Gaelic word tarnach meaning 'thunder-clap'.[47] Thunder Forest.

INTO THE FORESTS

The Royal Forest of Tarnaway, as it was once called, was originally part of the natural forest of Scotland. A report back in 1881 declared that the oak forest of Darnaway was 'acknowledged to be the finest in Scotland, and there are few which can compare with it anywhere in the British Isles'.[48] Much felling took place in the woods during the 15th and 16th centuries and the oak timber was used for ship building in Leith[49] and Inverness.[50] The oak was also used in the roofs of Inverness, Burghead,[51] Balvenie, Lochindorb, Ruthven[52] and Duffus[53] castles, as well as possibly Edinburgh and Stirling castles,[54] together with Spynie Palace and Elgin Cathedral.[55] During the lifetime of the 9th Earl of Moray (Francis, 1737–1810) upwards of 1,000,000 oak and 10,346,000 Scots pine were planted, plus 727,000 other hardwoods.[56] The Earl was appropriately known as 'The Tree Planter'.

A study conducted in 1997 of the sessile oaks (Quercus petraea Liebl) in the forest indicated ages of oak trees up to 727 years old. The oldest tree measured has a girth of 32 feet.[57] Many of these trees show signs of coppicing, and so we can only guess the age of the root structures. We are certainly talking about trees that would have been already growing when large mammals such as wolves and lynx, wild boar, moose and European beaver lived in the watershed. Maybe some of the roots even existed while bears roamed the river banks in search of salmon. The wildlife painter Archibald Thorburn wrote of the presence of bears in Scotland in his book Thorburn's Mammals:

The references made by ancient writers relating to the presence of the Bear in Great Britain during the Roman occupation of the country show that it was not uncommon in bygone days when animals from the Caledonian forests were transported to Rome to play their part in the arena. The Bear appears to have existed in Britain well into Saxon times, but the date of its extinction is uncertain.[58]

Indeed, European brown bears would have played an essential 'keystone' role in the ecosystem here all those centuries ago. Some fascinating recent studies along watersheds in British Columbia have demonstrated a correlation between salmon carcasses deposited by bears in forests and the proliferation of giant trees, with the salmon providing around half the nitrogen fixed by these old-growth trees.[59] Did bears contribute at one time to the growth of these ancient oaks along the River Findhorn?

Many of the finest oaks were carried away down river in the Great Moray Floods of 1829.[60] These oaks would have surrounded the jousting ground at the haugh field of the Meads of St. John. In 1390 the son of Robert II, Alexander Stewart, better known as 'The Wolf of Badenoch', was refused hospitality at Darnaway and banned from entering a tournament at the Meads on account of his being excommunicated by the church. In a huff, 'The Wolf' rode straight to Forres where he set fire to the town. Tournaments of this sort may have been frequent here during the Middle Ages as it is believed that there was once a cell of the Knights Hospitallers of St. John of Jerusalem at a location near to the Meads.[61]

Oaks are the true
Warriors of time
Their canyons of bark
Withstanding the wildest
Winds and weather

INTO THE FORESTS

As well as oaks, the forest comprises many species of native as well as exotic trees, and it is a pocket of Scotland rich in biological diversity. These species include alder, ash, rowan, elm, aspen, birch (silver and downy), lime, Spanish chestnut, hazel, holly, elder, blackthorn, willows, sycamore, beech, Scots pine, firs (grandis, noble, Norwegian, Douglas and silver), spruce, cedars and hemlock. The lower River Findhorn woods have been recognised for their ecological importance and are designated a Special Area of Conservation under the European Habitats Directive.

Species reintroduced to the forest include capercaillie and wild boar. The capercaillie were brought over from Scandinavia during the 1980s, and they are a rare but spectacular sight to behold as they cruise between the Scots pines. Wild boar have returned as part of a joint initiative between Altyre Estate and the Forestry Commission. The project demonstrates the important role that wild boar play in stimulating tree regeneration (particularly birch), as they work away in the undergrowth clearing the bracken and forming mounds of branches that in turn act as shelters for saplings. If ever you are lucky enough to see either of these two species in the forests, you can't help but notice how at home they look in this environment.

Waves of wind
Roll onto the translucent
Green shawl
Of the beeches
Their trunks
As if smeared
With grey clay
Wear the carvings
Of lovers' initials

37

WHITE RIVER

Tornadoes of mayflies
Fizz the air

A roe deer doe
With swollen belly
Slips her way
Down to a glade
Filled with leopards bane
And ferns

A series of forest tracks lead to the Ramflats where the cliffs, pillowing the river throughout this section, soar to their highest point. On the Darnaway side of the river herons used to nest in the old trees, but the heronry has long since been evacuated and the herons now nest elsewhere[62] The yellow broom and whin that grip the clifftops make clear views of the river a rarity from these heights. The sound of the rapids tumbling in the depths below rises from the gorge.

Now that it is well into the afternoon, I decide to base myself here for the night. It feels so good to drop the pack and to stretch my neck and shoulders. At least the pack will grow lighter each day as I eat into my food. Today's nine miles or so hasn't by any means been the longest day I've hiked before with a large pack, but muscles and feet take time to attune. I can feel the odd blister on a couple of toes, but apart from that the feet are in good shape. Blisters can create total hell on an expedition. I've certainly learned the hard way, and some of the first ski-touring trips I ever went on resulted in ski-boot agony. My preferred way to avoid blisters is to tape my heels with sports tape and sometimes Compede plasters – a bomb proof precaution. A great piece of advice I was once given was to take a break 20 minutes into your hike each morning to attend to hot spots on your feet, before your feet become to hot to mend.

I go down to the river to collect some water for a brew. I take the stove with me and find a flat rock some distance back from the water's edge for my makeshift kitchen. This evening's menu will be instant broccoli soup followed by pasta and pesto. Easy cooking. On mountaineering/backpack trips there is a limit to how much food you can carry, but if you rehydrate dried vegetables it is astonishing what can be produced. Food-carrying capacity is where a sea kayak and a canoe, however, come into their very own. There is nothing like serving up melon for breakfast on a remote beach a few days into a paddling trip.

I set up the tent a little later beside some aspen trees. Aspen are my favourite deciduous tree, and can be found in pockets throughout the lower Findhorn. They say that tincture of aspen can be taken to alleviate fear. I also remember someone telling me that there is a tradition in Finland of creating dugout canoes from large aspen trees. My tent is a few years old now, and I bought it in America when I was studying in North Carolina. A friend of mine slapped me on the back later that day and said 'Congratulations on purchasing your first home!' Prime real estate at US$140.

I awake the next morning to what is no less than an open-air jam session of birdsong. There is such variety in the music. A great spotted woodpecker plays drums.

Breakfast finished, gear packed away, I set off on day two. I hope to make it up to the Dulsie Bridge area by tonight. This morning is dry and fresh with a slight northerly breeze. Looking back downstream from a clearing in the forest, the tree canopy seems to glide like a magic carpet of green to the sea.

The mountains of Sutherland rise in the far distance marking the gateway to the north lands. This may be the last clear sight of the sea for many days now. Ducking under the needles of Sitka and whin where the track fades out, I continue upstream.

> Interlocking spurs
> Thick with larch
> And oak
> Alternate their way
> Up to Sluie

Sluie takes its name from the Gaelic word Sleagh meaning 'spear'. In olden times warriors used to cut their spears from these woods, hence 'The Place of the Spear'.[63] The pool at Sluie was for many years a major netting station on the river. So plentiful were the numbers of fish in the river that in the course of one evening in 1648 around 1,300 salmon were netted.[64] Around 1880, Darnaway Estate set up a business of fishing for salmon in the Sluie Lower Pool using boats and nets. Access to markets in the South was made possible through the opening of the Highland Railway with its nearby station at Dunphail.

The urgent need for timber during the First World War resulted in Canadian lumberjacks being recruited to fell the woods around Sluie[65] among other forests in the region. The Canadian approach to timber-felling differed starkly, it would seem, from a more ecologically and aesthetically sound tradition practised in the Highlands at that time:

The most unsightly relic is the shockingly large and wasteful stumps left sticking in the ground by the lumbermen. Perhaps the War was in too great a hurry to permit more time and care to be used in cutting down the trees. Perhaps Canadian methods were not easily adjusted to the more leisurely practice and the more artistic craftsmanship of Scots woodsmen. Whatever the reason, the stumps are horribly obvious, and will long be a nuisance to those who work in the plantations in times of peace.[66]

Whenever I see a woodland clear felled and a graveyard of tree stumps left in the ground among the debris, I often wonder how difficult it would be to bring back that 'leisurely practice' and 'artistic craftsmanship' to which Thomas Henderson referred. Today it would seem that much of the timber in Scotland is felled using giant timber harvesters, somewhat akin to combine harvesters. This form of timber extraction, whilst faster and more economically efficient for estates, is nevertheless brutish to the local ecology. When I think of the way in which forests are managed in the Alps, albeit using modern technology, there seems to be greater consideration given to minimising adverse visual and ecological impacts than in Scotland. Part of the issue is the fact that forest plantations in Scotland are viewed largely for their timber value, rather than for their environmental and amenity values.

What if we saw schemes introduced such as exist in Costa Rica whereby proprietors of woodland receive financial incentives for protecting the forest ecology, with the environmental value seen as a public value? rephrased: if the environmental value was to be seen as a planetary necessity. It has been suggested, in a similar way, that countries that contain rainforests – Brazil, Congo and Malaysia, for example – be paid sums of money from other international countries in order to block mass de-forestation, promote forest protection and thereby provide a vitally needed environmental service for preserving biodiversity

41

and encouraging carbon sinks. The point being that forests are such exceptionally precious resources, and the health of the planet – our health – is dependent upon their abundance.

Connected to the clear felling and stump abandonment is litter. Why is it – too often – that the likes of oil tanks and jerrycans are left to rust away at the sites of former timber extraction, instead of being taken away from the countryside? It would be wrong, of course, to say that this happens all the time. It would be unfair to direct this comment exclusively at the timber industry, when we find campsites used by outdoor enthusiasts despoiled by litter and water sources contaminated. Take the base camp of Mount Everest – a place that should inspire respect for the natural world, but which is strewn with litter from mountain expeditions. A mountaineering friend of mine once suggested that unless a climbing party packs out all the litter that they bring into a mountain environment, then any summit success they have achieved should not count.

'Leave-no-trace', as outdoor schools advocate, particularly in North America (such as the National Outdoor Leadership School, NOLS, Outward Bound and Canadian Outdoor Leadership Training, COLT). There is less emphasis on leave-no-trace camping in outdoor education in the UK, just as, I have found, there is less focus on sound camping skills compared to the 'hard', technical skills of disciplines such as climbing and kayaking. Part of the effect is that outdoor enthusiasts may never learn how to move within a natural environment 'softly' and with minimum impact – thus remaining essentially separated from the environment in which they find themselves. Another consequence of not learning respect for the natural world is that the ego can swell with the outdoor practitioner erroneously believing that they are 'superior' to the environment. A false sense of security can in turn lead to inaccurate risk assessment of natural features (whitewater, avalanche zones, weather etc.). When we go lightly, by contrast, we may find the Earth's secrets revealed.

It amazes me when people manage to drive fridge-freezers miles into the countryside to some remote location (or did they simply drop out of the sky?) – the effort involved to fly-tip so remotely must be considerable. It's not a widely publicised fact (but something that local authorities are mandated to advertise) that litterers can face fines of up to £2,500 under the Environmental Protection Act 1990. In Yosemite National Park in California I recall the upper cap for littering being a cool $1,000 – enough to make someone think twice before garlanding the verges with rubbish. Should taxes be spent on employing teams to clean up litter in the countryside? The danger is that this kind of approach comes straight out of the School of the Sticking Plaster Mentality. Sticking plasters work for a limited period, but a more durable approach is needed. Ultimately it takes strength of community and a love of place to combat the litter problem. We also need to rethink radically the whole concept of waste so that everything we produce is reused and recycled, and not just recycled but up-cycled so that something's value is never lost[67] Whereas I think it's fair to say that Scotland lags behind many of its European neighbours when it comes to recycling, one excellent example of creative recycling and community waste management is the Moray Waste Busters project on the outskirts of Forres.

Returning to forestry for a moment, there are, thank goodness, moves throughout the country where native trees are being encouraged, and sound silvicultural practices are being promoted[68] Whilst there are some shocking examples of poor forestry management within the watershed of the River Findhorn, there are, nevertheless, some truly skilled and knowledgeable foresters throughout the area.

At Sluie the geology of the River Findhorn changes from Old Red Sandstone to a mixture of gneiss and granite. From here to Dulsie Bridge the river tightens into a breathtaking series of short pools, spouts and falls like nowhere else in Scotland. The young Queen Victoria is said to have marvelled at the sight of the rapids barrelling over the rocks here, and one of the vistas in this section is referred to as the Princess View.[69] The river in this cliff section ranges from five to 30 feet across, with the cliffs rising at least 100 feet high. There are some wider pools such as at Sluie itself, but generally the river concentrates into a narrow yet very deep line through the rock.

Until a few years ago my main contact with the river was through fly fishing, when I would look upon a pool with an eye to where a salmon might be lying. But nowadays with my principal river passion being canoeing, the first instinct upon looking at a stretch of water is to work out the line a rapid might be run. Both perspectives increase your understanding of a river, and both sets of skills – fishing and paddling – are all part of becoming a 'river person'.

There is an ominous roar in the canyon below. This section of river from Randolph's Leap to Sluie forms the most technically challenging stretch of water for paddling on the River Findhorn. You'd struggle to paddle a standard 15-16ft canoe through this grade 4 (5 in high water) section, although a shorter, more specialised whitewater canoe (complete with extra buoyancy) would provide an unforgettable experience. For kayakers, this section is one of the finest in Scotland, not simply for the actual rapids, but also for the sense of remoteness experienced in the canyon.

Haugh fields of Highland cattle bordered by the sinewy limbs of beech trees mark the way up to Logie. Logie ('The Hollow') sits in a natural amphitheatre where the steading has been transformed into a prize-winning centre featuring local crafts, an art gallery, a garden centre and the watershed's best café, amongst other things. It is an excellent example of how local business can be stimulated and supported by a community of enterprise.

As a child at Logie Primary School I remember going for walks through the beech woods here and being captivated by the summer canopy and autumn carpet of the leaves. I also recall from these walks what seemed like the world's longest ascent climbing up the Carrbridge road that leads back to the top of the brae. It was an idyllic location to go to school. Logie, like a number of the rural primary schools in Moray, has been faced with possible closure in recent years. Threat of closure tends to be based on economics rather than a lack of good educational standards. As it happens, Logie's education is of such a high standard that a recent HMI school inspection report gave Logie glowing praise. National government educational policy as implemented by local government has argued that Logie, purportedly, has the capacity for more pupils than are currently in attendance, but, because the school only has a certain percentage of this 'optimum' number, it does not in turn demonstrate a wise use of government funds. Yet as soon as a school is faced with closure, it is the natural reaction of some parents to want to jump ship and relocate their children in a school with greater prospects of remaining open, so reducing further the numbers at the school and weakening its position.

Schools such as Logie cannot sustain such intense scrutiny without at some point buckling under the pressure, which is why they must be treated differently by government when compared to urban schools that are easier to fill, and their role in the rural community beyond being simply schools must be fully acknowledged and quantified in the economic analysis. In a place such as Logie, where the school serves the rural communities of Altyre and Dunphail in addition to Logie, and where there is no longer a village shop/post office as there once was, the school becomes the very focal point of community life.

If you take front page news coverage as a yardstick, it is fair to say that the public has become far more receptive to environmental issues than was the case before the millennium. How we deal with these issues as a society presents the greatest challenge humanity has ever had to face collectively. If children are the future decision makers, then environmental education must be taught at the earliest stage of a person's development. For this reason alone, educational establishments that provide children with direct contact with the natural world are invaluable. In terms of development of rural areas – such as the Highlands – it is crucial that children grow up to see the inherent values of the countryside, and why there is worth in remaining in such communities rather than necessarily moving away to the bright lights of cities.

Just upstream from Logie the River Divie ('The Black Goddess') joins the River Findhorn. The Divie rises in the hills beyond Feakirk, and connects with the River Dorback ('The Minnow') that drains Lochinborb and the ground to the east of the Knock of Braemoray. Close to the 'Meeting of the Waters' of the Findhorn and Divie lies the site of an ancient Pictish fortress.

INTO THE FORESTS

Whether the rivers were actually named by the Picts remains unclear. However, someone at some time must have sensed the black meeting the white. Yin meeting yang. The outcrop of rock at the point where the two rivers meet provides a welcome spot to rest before moving on to Randolph's Leap and beyond.

CHAPTER THREE

The Salmon

'Through the hollows and valleys of the sea the fresh water penetrated, thinning out as it went, but ever being pressed and increased from behind, until at last its influence touched the gills of the restless fish and they found refreshment therein, the sting of excitement.'

Neil Gunn, Highland River[70]

After half an hour of resting in the morning sunlight, watching a heron studying the river, I resume the journey upstream. A well-trodden path leads past the thundering rapids below Randolph's Leap. Here the water boils and surges the colour of caramel. Tree trunks jettisoned by spates lie at awkward angles across the far bank. Amidst the fury of the water, the rocks mid-stream are patterned with concentric, harmonious lines.

Randolph's Leap is a misnomer because it was Alastair Comyn (rather than Randolph) who made the jump across the chasm from left bank to right. I have often thought how Mr Comyn might have escaped Randolph's men at Darnaway more successfully, instead of meeting the tragic end of being smoked to death in the Cave of Slock-nan'cean near the Divie.[71] For years I imagined a 'Butch Cassidy and the Sundance Kid' approach of leaping into the river and floating away to freedom, but the rapids below would have posed a major problem.

If only he had had his trusty kayak tethered to the bank, he might have evaded his foes and reached Findhorn Bay in time for tea.

Positioned at some 50 feet above the low-water level, a cairn at Randolph's Leap marks the height to which the river rose during the Great Moray Floods of 1829. It is unimaginable just how phenomenal – if not terrifying – the spectacle and noise of the river must have been to those nearby on that day.

Along the track from Randolph's Leap upriver to Daltulich Bridge stand the most gigantic Douglas firs. Like the paintings of Giant Redwoods by Albert Bierstadt in the late 19th century, these trees seem to glow with life. It is hard to believe, given the fact that the Scottish botanist David Douglas sent the first Douglas fir seeds from the west coast of North America to England in 1827[72] that these trees could have reached such a size in less than 200 years.

Following the fishing track upstream where the river straightens its course for about half a mile, the path traverses a landslide before descending to a beach where the rapids rumble by. Up and around the bend stands Daltulich Bridge, dividing the downstream Parish of Edinkillie ('The Face of the Wood') from the upstream Parish of Ardclach ('Stony High Ground'). It also marks the boundary between Moray and Nairnshire. The construction of the current bridge at Daltulich ('Field of the Hill') was a second attempt by the same contractor after his first effort collapsed – and you can only imagine what a bad day at work that must have been.

After crossing to the left bank at Coulmony, you come across a truly stunning copper beech. Its leaves seem to tumble like ruby raindrops.

WHITE RIVER

Oyster catchers
Pipe a tune
Belted Galloways
Graze the haugh
Birds and beasts
In black and white

A fisherman on the far bank Spey-casts into the stream. Spey-casting: one of life's transcendental motions. You can go for days without so much as a bite at the end of your line, and still remain ensconced in its meditative swirl. That five-beat rhythm of lifting the rod and line so that the fly remains in the water, looping a lasso-like circle, and then shooting the line out towards the treetops on the opposite bank. The secret is about keeping tension on the line so that energy is transferred throughout the cast with maximum efficiency, releasing the line across the water with punch. Then the two-step shuffle downstream to the next cast.

I remember being taught at the age of around ten by the late Hugh MacBean from Relugas – a master fly fisherman. He maintained that if I wanted to be a true fly fisher, I had to learn to cast with both right and left shoulders, so that the body was always turned downriver. There are variations on the cast such as the Double-Spey where you carve a giant figure of eight in the air, which is especially useful when the wind blows upstream. Then there are those mind-bogglingly complex casts like the Snake, which only exceptional ghillies ever seem to unfurl with ease. Spey-casting is at once useful in that you lessen the chance of losing a fly in the alder trees behind. It also minimises back and shoulder pain, and so you can fish for even longer into the evening shadows.

THE SALMON

What sets apart fishing on the Findhorn from many other famous salmon rivers in the Highlands is that you don't need to able to cast more than 30 yards to cover the water, which means you don't really need to wade either. The pools are often so narrow and gnarly that you are better wearing a pair of running shoes, and instead perching upon a rock and simply improvising styles of casting to adapt to the geography.

Given the beauty and grace of fly fishing, I've never really understood the attraction of spinning (other than the fact that you might catch more fish and that it is easier to cast). There is also a whole anthropology of fly-tying from around the world – designs, colours and species' feathers that combine to recall a day on the water, or which come together on a long winter's evening when the dream of a season of abundant catches stirs hope.

Maybe it was Norman MacLean's story A River Runs Through It about fishing in Montana that created the fly fishing over spinning bias in me at an early age. MacLean writes of Jesus' disciples all being fishermen, and that all the best fishermen on the Sea of Galilee were fly fishermen with John, Jesus' favourite, being a dry-fly fisherman.[73]

Charles St. John, the sportsman and naturalist who came to know the Findhorn intimately, mocked the type of people that fish the Findhorn with all their pomp and excessive trimmings:[74]

I have been much amused by seeing an elderly, placid-looking London gentleman, who was staying at Forres for the purpose of fishing the Findhorn. He arrives at the river's edge at a comfortable noon-day hour, accompanied by his lady and a footman splendid in blue and red, who carries camp-stools, books, fishing tackle, and last, though not least, a most voluminous luncheon. Daily this party make their appearance at a certain pool, and while the old gentleman, seated at his ease on his camp-stool close to the water, with spectacles and broad-brimmed hat, fishes away with the well known perseverance and skill of a Thames angler, his lady reads her book on one side, whilst on the other the red-legged footman either prepares the luncheon or holds in readiness the well-stocked fly-book of his master. Very different would be the description given of our Scotch fishing by one who thus practices the gentle craft on the level grassy banks of the lower pools of the Findhorn, from that of the sportsman who seeks the salmon over the rugged passes of the rocks which overhang the deep black pools and rushing torrents of the same river between Dulsie Bridge and the Heronry.

There is a distinction, as St. John points out, between a fisher who comes to the river intent on a grand picnic, and the fisher who seeks above all a sense of immersion in wild nature and solitude from civilisation. Ernest Hemingway summed up the tone of the latter fishing experience in his short story Big Two-Hearted River,[75] where the main character heads off to the backcountry of Michigan on a solo camping trip to fish for trout. Hemingway captured that essence like no other, and revealed the tonic of the wild that fishing can provide. Stripped away from all the trappings of civilisation, and pared down to its bare essential, fly fishing encapsulates a tangible purity. There is ruggedness, yet there is also finesse. For those in need of escape from the ennui of modern city life (as John Buchan once described in his classic tale, John MacNab), a fishing trip to a wild Highland river or loch may be just what the doctor ordered. Simple, spontaneous and spiritual.

THE SALMON

Standing on a rock
Dewy Spring morning
Casting out onto rapids
A squadron of mergansers
Strikes up the canyon
Birch and aspen leaves
Swell the tree canopy
Above a splash
Of flashing silver

I fish less today than I used to, and it's largely because of the widespread decline in salmon catches around Scotland. Ironically, the less I've fished, the more I've become fascinated by the sheer wonder of Atlantic salmon. Take their ability to return to the exact place of their birth to spawn. This precise navigation and focus on perpetuating the cycle of life is nothing short of miraculous. Consider the obstacles a salmon may face both in the river and at sea in its journey to and from the feeding grounds off Greenland and the Faeroe Islands. With wild Atlantic salmon numbers hinting at a possible extinction of the species in the North Atlantic, conservation work to help restore wild salmon runs in the River Findhorn and throughout Scotland is now more vital than ever.

Because grilse (salmon that return to spawn in rivers after only one winter feeding at sea) numbers in Scotland have remained relatively consistent since the 1950s[76] many people believe that there is no real threat to the health of wild salmon stocks. The extraordinary optimism that many fishermen possess (convinced that today really is their lucky day) can also create a block in acknowledging the real reasons for a decline in the numbers of multi-sea-winter salmon.

If we look at just some of the facts, however, the pattern of decline is alarming. Wild salmon catches in the North Atlantic basin are down by some 80% in the past 25 years.[77] Wild Atlantic salmon populations in one-third of rivers in North America and Europe are endangered[78] and have already disappeared completely from 309 river systems in Europe and North America. Stocks are on the brink of extinction in Portugal, Estonia, Poland, the United States and the Southern parts of Canada. Ninety per cent of healthy populations are found in only four countries, i.e. Norway, Iceland, Ireland and Scotland, and 85% of populations outside these four countries are considered vulnerable, endangered or critical.[79]

Compared to the peak catches during the post-war years of the 1960s and 1970s, the overall level of wild salmon (including grilse) returning to Scottish rivers is down by around one-third to a half.[80] When we look at the combined number of multi-sea-winter salmon and grilse caught in the River Findhorn, records show that there has been a drop from 14,475 in 1983 to 1,601 in the year 2000; sea trout catches in the River Findhorn have also declined over the same time span dropping from 1,048 in 1983 to 307 in 2000.[81] The latest statistics on combined catches of grilse and salmon for the river were 3,362 in 2004, and 2,374 in 2005 – both improvements on the number caught in 2000, but nevertheless significantly less than the numbers caught in the early 1980s.[82]

While the general condition of wild stocks in Scottish rivers remains comparatively healthy despite a considerable drop in numbers of multi-winter salmon, if stocks collapse throughout much of the Atlantic region then increased pressure will mount upon wild salmon of Scottish origin. The result of such ecological damage could mean an adverse economic impact for many rural communities throughout Scotland, not to mention a weakening of cultural character.

The significance of these statistics moves to another level when we consider that the Atlantic salmon is an 'indicator' species. The concept of an indicator species is comparable to a canary in a mineshaft – it is a litmus test, so to speak, of the health of the natural environment. Part of the reason for this indicator status is that the Atlantic salmon is anadromous – in other words it is born in freshwater, does most of its growing at sea, and then returns to the river of its birth to spawn. Moreover, the salmon journeys through a variety of habitats across a vast geographical range. The other reason for its indicator qualification is that the environmental requirements of salmon are especially demanding: in order to complete their life cycle, Atlantic salmon demand unobstructed access to well-oxygenated, unpolluted rivers, well supplied with clear, cool, relatively silt-free water, and with a range of bed types that provides both spawning and rearing opportunities.[83] At sea, they require adequate levels of secondary production at the Atlantic Ocean/Arctic interface, and freedom from coastal pollution (including aquaculture), and from directed and accidental exploitation by fishing at unsustainable rates. A decline in wild salmon stocks is a sure sign, therefore, that the natural world of the North Atlantic is in poor condition.

How might we prevent the ecological catastrophe of a collapse in the wild salmon population from taking place? How might we restore wild salmon stocks in Scottish rivers and throughout the North Atlantic to former levels of abundance? How, indeed, might we work to improve the health of the natural environment in the Atlantic basin of which we are part?

There is no single, straightforward answer to the wild salmon debate. The issue is multi-faceted and involves many interrelating factors. Given the anadromous nature of salmon there are threats in fresh water, during first entry into the marine environment and in the open seas. Nevertheless, perhaps the best way forward is to identify the various threats to wild salmon survival, seven of which I consider to be the major ones that require closer consideration: hydro generation schemes, coniferous afforestation, agriculture, aquaculture, human exploitation, climate change and predators.

Hydro schemes can cause damage to salmon and salmon eggs whenever there are surges of water through compensation flows and freshet releases. Also some projects (such as in the upper tributaries of the River Spey) divert water from one catchment to another for industrial reasons and so may exacerbate low water levels. Dams can present difficulty to adult salmon in their passage upstream and so block access to headwaters, and smolts may find their downstream migration impeded. Fortunately there are no such dams on the River Findhorn.

The planting of coniferous trees has a number of effects upon salmon. This practice may increase erosion and cause excess silt input in rivers. This silt can blanket vital gravel beds that are required for spawning. In areas of poor base geology and soil types, such afforestation exacerbates acidification, which can cause problems to salmon stocks[84] Conifer plantations are also thought to increase water loss through evapotranspiration, in turn altering the nature of water discharge into rivers[85]

Intensive arable farming that involves ploughing in autumn may cause harm to salmon, when topsoils are exposed to rainfall and are disturbed and thus lead to river siltation. There may also be direct pollution to the river system from agro-chemicals, as well as eutrophication caused through artificial nutrients[86] Livestock that graze river banks can contribute to bank erosion, augmenting siltation as well as widening the river (which can create shallower streams and remove deep water habitats).[87]

Commercial salmon farming is thought to impact upon wild salmon stocks in a number of ways. First of all it has been suggested that the relationship between sea lice concentrations associated with salmon farming and the damage inflicted by sea lice upon sea trout and wild salmon (post smolts) is a link 'beyond reasonable doubt'.[88] Secondly, salmon farming is thought to encourage disease in wild salmon, such as furunculosis, salmon anaemia, and Gyrodactylus salaris.[89] Another impact from aquaculture is the possibility of pollution of sea water in sea lochs and fjords from factors such as uneaten food, fish faeces and medications including antibiotics. A further threat to wild salmon is the possibility of interbreeding with escapees from farms, which in turn dilutes the genetic characteristics of wild stocks originating from a specific river.

Salmon returning to rivers are caught by rod and line, with rod fisheries in Scotland in 1995 being valued at an estimated net economic worth of around £350 million. Indeed salmon anglers in Scotland are thought to bring some £70 million pounds per annum to the Scottish economy, including indirect effects.[90] Understandably, there is pressure that rivers perform well. However, when wild stocks are low it is imperative that critical spawning stocks are not damaged.

There is also pressure from net fisheries at sea. Driftnetting is now largely subject to regulation by the North Atlantic Salmon Conservation Organisation (NASCO), and so although the practice still continues off Ireland and off the north-east coast of England the overall situation throughout the North Atlantic has been brought under stricter control. There is also evidence of an impact on wild salmon stocks from inclusion in the by-catches of pelagic fisheries, in particular from mackerel and herring fishing.[91]

Evidence suggests a link between the effects of climate change upon ocean temperatures and currents and the pattern of a ubiquitous decline in the marine survival rates of wild salmon.[92] Another effect of climate change is the prevalence of extreme rainfall that causes flooding and as a result washes out 'redds' (salmon beds). Such fluctuating conditions mean that drought is experienced more frequently, which may result in a loss to juvenile salmon riffle habitats.[93] In other words the unpredictable weather patterns tend to hinge upon extremes rather than a steady medium.

Grey seals have come under increasing scrutiny for their impact upon wild salmon numbers. However, a number of studies state that there is little evidence to support such a correlation, and that seals play less of an inflicting role than has been portrayed by the media in recent times.[94] The boom in aquaculture in the past few decades may play some part in the rise of seals around Scottish waters with 137,000 tonnes of farmed salmon produced in the year 2000 – a rise in quantity by a factor of ten over a twelve year period from 1988.[95] This rise in farmed salmon coupled with the crash of cod stocks[96] around the North Atlantic may have led to a change in seal diets. Also, birds such as great cormorants, red-breasted mergansers and goosander are thought to have an impact on wild stocks by preying upon juvenile salmon in particular.

Crossing the river again at Logie Bridge on the Grantown-on-Spey to Nairn road, you enter Glenferness ('The Glen of the Waterfall of the Alders'). 'I know no river scenery,' wrote Sir Thomas Dick Lauder of Relugas in Highland Legends, 'in Great Britain at all to be compared in sublimity to that of the Findhorn about Ferness. Indeed, it rises more into that great scale of grandeur exhibited by some of the Swiss gorges than anything I have ever met with at home.'[97]

I take my lunch break beneath some bird cherry trees. There's some pita bread I want to eat sooner rather than later, and so decide that its match is some mushroom paté from a tube. A friend once introduced me to the wonders of mushroom paté in a tube, a backcountry essential, on the summit of Suilven in Inverpolly a few years back. We spent three days in the Inverpolly wilderness. After launching the canoe north of Elfin, we made our way into Loch Veyatie and battled against a strong head wind for a good few hours. Eventually we set up camp on an isthmus along the shore of Fionn Loch beneath the grandeur that is Suilven. Some describe Suilven as a hog's back or a giant sugar loaf. Like all of the other Inverpolly mountains – Quinag, Cannich, Cul Mor, Cul Beg and Stac Pollaidh – Suilven stands in its own space, unshrouded by other peaks. Like masterpieces in an art gallery, there is sufficient room for each Inverpolly mountain to make its own individual statement.

The next morning we approached the mountain from the south and climbed through cloud to its bealach, or saddle. The west summit of Suilven is a flat, grassy expanse. We took a seat facing south, although visibility was less than thirty feet. At times like those you sometimes wonder why we exert ourselves, travelling into remote areas and climbing mountains, only to have no view from the top. Then came the mushroom paté. As the first round of oatcakes were coated in this space-food, the cloud cover began to fragment. At first, glimpses of distant heather. Piece by piece the jigsaw of cloud layers was removed until the expanse of the Inverpolly wilds stretched out around us. The northern corries of Cul Mor, the islands of Loch Sionascaig, the gargoyle pinnacles of Stac Pollaidh, the cluster of the Summer Isles, the harbour at Lochinver and the trident peak of Quinag.

Sometimes we have to sit and wait for the gift to arrive. It is too easy to rush. Those hell bent on reaching the summit and racing back down may forget to enjoy the wonder. Each to their own. We all have different reasons and philosophies for going into the outdoors. For some it is conquest. For others it is reverence.

Today's entrée of pita and mushroom paté is followed by a raspberry Ma Baker bar – the finest flapjack I have yet discovered – and washed down with a cup of tea. Energy levels are restored for the afternoon's stint through Glenferness.

The path often disappears into a carpet of Broad Buckler, Brittle Bladder and Hard Shield ferns.[98] Sometimes you have to leave the shade of the alders and instead scramble over the granite rocks washed up beside the narrow channel of the fast-moving current. At one point both the path and the rocks run out and there is no other way forward. You end up having to scale a steep ravine thick with slippery Mountain Melick grass. Without a heavy pack this wouldn't be much of a problem, but then extra weight makes it an effort. Fortunately there is the odd birch up the slope that I can reach to pull me up. At the top of the slope I flop my body over the edge like a seal lurching onto a sandbank. Certainly no points from the judges for style, and few if any for technical merit.

I continue on through the woods in sight of the river as it bounces its way down through the rocky pools.

Giant fallen pine
Spiders at Tomnarroch Burn
Moss covered legs
Dappled
With flecks of sunlight

THE SALMON

Elder blossom
Beaconing
Through shadowy hues
Darker
Than downriver greens

Across the water by the river's edge sits the Parish Church of Ardclach. Built far from the level of the road on the left bank, its location was a compromise between the rival claims of the parishioners on the north and south banks. High on the hill beyond the church stands a bell-tower. Legend has it that the bell was rung as a warning for the locals to hide their cattle whenever 'Highland caterans' from Strathdearn approached from upstream. The bell was eventually cut down by reivers and thrown into the river.[99]

A couple of roe deer graze in the long field that leads to Dalnaheiglish Wood. Here stand Douglas firs with those signature cracks that run down their trunks, as if clawed by a bear scraping for honey. A forestry track leads through a carpet of primroses down to the pool at Daltra, where the spur on the far bank once formed an island occupied by a hermit of the early Columban church.[100]

Having never been to this section of the river before, there is that sense of strange familiar. The river remains the same colour, but the physicalities of the river's banks are different from downstream. There is greater jaggedness in the rocks, but a more intricate line danced by the water.

Returning to the various major threats that face wild salmon – hydro-electric schemes, coniferous afforestation, intensive agriculture, aquaculture, human exploitation, climate change, and predators – whilst they might seem independent issues, closer analysis reveals that all are consequences of the same economic model. Free market capitalism, as this system is sometimes called, champions a short-term economic fix at all costs. Promulgated by treaties such as the European Union (EU), the North American Free Trade Agreement (NAFTA) and by the Bretton Woods institutions of the World Bank, the International Monetary Fund (IMF) and the World Trade Organisation (WTO), this model tends to be referred to worldwide as globalisation.

The underlying economic theory that legitimises the global economy has, through time, been misinterpreted and misused. Whereas Adam Smith in The Wealth of Nations[101] sought ways to end the state protection of business monopolies through his concepts of capitalism, today we are witnessing the protection of transnational corporate monopolies via WTO laws, such as the TRIPs (Trade Related Aspects of International Property Rights) and the TBT (Technical Barriers to Trade) agreements. In other words, even though proponents of a global economy tend to justify their actions by relying upon Adam Smith's economic principles, they instead apply them in the directly opposite manner and with the directly opposite goals that Smith advocated. In fact, Adam Smith intended that capital would be rooted in a particular place, the reason being that there has to be the social and moral fabric of a community in which people know one another for the 'invisible hand' of the market to work effectively. The current free market, capitalist/globalisation, economic-political model can be categorised, however, by the following assumptions:[102]

- humans are motivated by self-interest, expressed primarily through the quest for financial gain;

THE SALMON

- the action that yields the greatest financial return to the individual or firm is the one that is most beneficial to society;
- competitive behaviour is more rational for the individual and the firm and more beneficial to society than cooperative behaviour;
- human progress is best measured by increases in the value of what the members of society consume, and those who consume the most contribute the most to that progress;
- competitive advantage is gained when bigger, more efficient plants manufacture more products for sale to expanding markets;
- growth in total output (GDP) maximises human well-being;
- and concerns for a healthy environment are important but must be balanced against the requirements of economic growth, if a high standard of living is to be maintained.

Applying the above principles to the threats facing wild salmon, it becomes evident that economic growth created through aquaculture or coniferous afforestation can be justified even if they pollute the natural environment. The notion that whatever practice yields the greatest financial return is the most beneficial to society is a premise that supports hydro-electric dams and the European Union's Common Fisheries Policies (CFP), regardless of the fact that salmon runs may be blocked, or that cod stocks are fished to the brink of extinction. The belief that maximum consumption signals progress is a simple justification for human exploitation. The assumption that humans are primarily driven by self-interest is a useful excuse for the unravelling of the cooperative fabric of rural communities. Climate change is aggravated by the acceleration of such trade and its inherent requirements for transportation across the globe.

Essentially such an economic system is digging its own grave. Not only does it ignore the worth of human capital – such as labour, intelligence and culture – but also it disregards the natural capital of resources, living systems and ecosystems. Through misguided accounting the conventional capitalist-globalisation model liquidates its capital and erroneously refers to it as income.[103] The natural environment is not an optional second-class factor of economic theory, but is the very basis of economics. Without a natural environment, there can be no economics.

CHAPTER FOUR

Leven's Gorge

'Black canyons where the rapids rip and roar'
Robert Service, 'The Call of the Wild'[104]

Resting on a beach amidst the green denseness of the forest, staring out across the cola water, I notice a small head rise from the surface. It dips, followed by the perfect arch of its back and the splashless grace of its tail. The otter then rises further upstream, the hair at the back of its neck all spiked. After circling the pool, writhing and tumbling in the sunlit water, it disappears out of sight. It is always such a treat to see an otter, and I've seen more on the West Coast around places like Knoydart and Skye than along the River Findhorn. As a species they are afforded the fullest legal protection in Europe under the European Habitats Directive.

There is a delicious sense of separation from the modern world here, created not so much by the actual distance from roads and houses, as by the fact that the woodland has been allowed to unfurl to a fullness.

I keep thinking about the subject of salmon, and how the current model of globalisation limits so many conservation measures. What if we had a system that as a foundation block acknowledged the importance of natural capital? One that encouraged resource productivity and the protection of biological diversity, instead of something which both directly and collaterally diminishes the planet's environmental systems. A model that radically reappraised the link between a healthy environment and a vibrant economy.

Indigenous cultures throughout time around the North Atlantic, such as the ancient Picts of Scotland, modern day Sami of Scandinavia or Inuit of Greenland, considered salmon central to their existence and culture.[105] Which makes me wonder what might happen if we, instead of placing economic emphasis upon Gross Domestic Product (GDP), used instead the health of wild salmon runs as an economic indicator, reorientating our entire economy and political structure around restoring wild salmon? This essentially means conserving and restoring anything that is beneficial to salmon, and abandoning any practices that could damage the natural capital of wild stocks.

Using salmon as our economic (as well as ecological) indicator, could we possibly navigate from crisis to abundance, from disconnection to reconnection? Seth Zuckerman describes in his book Salmon Nation[106] how by using the salmon's guidance we can learn to relate to the natural world. If we are to make a major shift in the way our economy protects the likes of salmon, then we have to change before wild stocks pass beyond a point of no return – which in turn makes Scotland's wild salmon heritage an even more valuable genetic resource for the North Atlantic basin.

If we were to apply the test of 'is it good for salmon' as our yardstick for economic activity, then the resulting picture might look as follows:

There would be an end to any hydro-electric dams that blocked salmon runs, or which caused wash-out of redds through freshet release. There would also be an end to any forms of power that contribute to climate change, such as fossil fuels. Instead, alternatives such as solar, biomass, micro-wind, offshore wind and wave power might be harnessed, as well as motor vehicles such as the Hypercar[107] that run from hybrid fuel and hydrogen cell technologies.

We would see a ban on chemical pesticides and synthetic fertilisers and nutrients, and a move towards widescale organic methods. This would also encourage greater employment. In order to combat climate change, unnecessary international trade of products that can be homespun would be stopped, for example the practice of both exporting and importing milk from and to the UK.

Any aquaculture would be more community/locally owned by stakeholders with a vested interest in protecting their local, marine environment, instead of ownership by a handful of multinationals whose principal aim is the maximisation of financial profits. Organic aquaculture – if genuinely possible – without the use of chemicals would also be encouraged.

In order to stimulate genuine sustainable fishery development, the recovery of pelagic and whitefish fisheries must be a priority. Statistics show that for every job offshore, four jobs are created inland.[108] Again this could be community based so that people take care of the commons, harvesting the natural income and safeguarding the natural capital. A re-emergence of off-shore fisheries might also detract seal attention away from salmon and towards cod, and thereby help boost salmon numbers.

The blanket planting of non-native conifers such as Sitka spruce and Lodgepole pine near water sources would end, and instead deciduous hardwoods would be encouraged. Such hardwoods would provide insect food, shade, bank stability, silt control, and would help retain water in the ground promoting springs to make river flow more regular and thus help prevent flooding.[109] Reforestation would encourage biological diversity through habitat creation, and, in order to encourage forest regeneration, species such as wild boar and beaver would be reintroduced. The planting and growth of significant numbers of hardwoods would help combat CO_2 emissions that contribute towards climate change. Resource productivity such as forestry provides a basis for higher employment levels and meaningful jobs.[110]

Prioritising the restoration of wild salmon stocks at economic and political levels, together with the social benefits of more meaningful employment and community stability, would foster a greater respect for the natural environment and so deepen cultural awareness and identity. As a result, humans would be less prone to exploiting natural resources but would treat wild salmon with the reverence of kinship – an insurance against the depletion of natural capital. However, a greater abundance of salmon could support more salmon fishing, thereby boosting tourism and so securing and creating employment in areas such as the hotel industry, ghillieing, salmon smokeries, fish tackle shops and so on.

After what must be quarter of an hour, I notice the same little head breaking the water's surface just downstream. The otter then dives to explore the underwater world, before appearing up in the neck of the pool in an eddy. Has it got a fish? I cannot see from this angle. The otter looks about and then scurries up the far bank over the rocks and sand onto the grass. There it pauses briefly to shake the water from its pelt. There is no fish after all. It scuttles along the bank for ten yards, and then disappears into the undergrowth out of sight.

The sky above the gorge here provides only a snapshot of the outside world, as fragmented cumulus clouds coast over from what must be the north west (at least, that is my conclusion with the sun being in its southern reaches at this time of day). I wonder what tomorrow's weather will bring. Today has remained dry, which is a blessing.

Setting off back upstream from the beach, I keep working away in my mind at this notion of local economies instead of a global economy. Local economies require local politics and autonomy from large centralised institutions such as the European Union. It is interesting, therefore, (and perhaps without coincidence) that recent moves towards local economies have been termed as 'watershed economics', or bioregionalism. As Kirkpatrick Sale describes in his essay 'Principles of Bioregionalism', bioregional economies seek to protect and restore their natural resources and not allow them to diminish. Bioregional economies also try to achieve a level of production determined by need and based upon a system of exchange, rather than focussing upon constant production and excess consumption.[111]

Bioregionalism encourages differentiation and discourages homogenisation. It embraces the vernacular. You only need drive that spectacular backroad journey from Inverness to Perth, via Tomintoul and Braemar – taking in river valleys such as the Nairn, Findhorn, Dulnain, Spey, Avon, (the Deveron, too, for a very worthwhile detour), Don, Cauld, Dee, Isla and Tay – to realise how the trees vary, the rocks change, how each valley 'feels' distinctive with its own identity, how the vernacular architecture changes (e.g. dormer window design), and how fiddle music differs in each location.

Looking at watershed restoration work in particular, it is useful to recognise events in the Pacific North West of the United States and Canada to see what can be achieved by such a change.

In 1998, some 200 watershed restoration groups were at work between California and British Columbia, compared to 94 in 1989.[112] The efforts to restore salmon habitats in watersheds – cabling logs to stream beds to provide shelter for salmon, purchasing irrigation rights to keep water in the rivers during dry summer months, fencing livestock away from river banks – has strengthened a connection to place in the people involved. The annual return of salmon has given reason to celebrate, a rhythm that can be not just culturally enriching but ecologically nourishing for dependent ecosystems.[113] Festivals such as the Wild Olympic Salmon festival in Chimacum, Washington State, are ways for humans to reconnect to the natural world and strengthen cultural identity.

In terms of economics, Seth Zuckerman describes in 'Toward a New Salmon Economy'[114] that people in the Pacific North West who are aware of salmon conservation are making efforts to develop ways that allow a harvest from the land yet at the same time rebuilding the land's productive capacity. One innovative concept being used in the Pacific North West to raise awareness of the industrial impacts on salmon and to reward and distinguish producers who seek to minimise their ecological footprint is the use of labelling programs. Labels such as 'Salmon Safe' and 'Fish Friendly' are being applied to industries as broad as electricity and wine. The possibilities of rewarding ecologically conscious industries in Scotland in such a way, from aquaculture to organic agriculture to whisky distilleries, could be equally beneficial both to wild salmon and to the marketability of quality products.

Approaching the Rock Walk at Glenferness, steep banks of Scots pine and silver birch soar two hundred feet up from the river. A small waterfall runs its white line over the rock into the black water of the canyon. Upon the surface of the peaty coloured water towards the neck of the pool here, white foam forms continually shifting circular patterns. Was this movement the inspiration behind Celtic art?

> From around the bend
> Comes the baritone
> Charge
> Of unstoppable
> White water

At the top end of the Rock Walk roars the switchback rapid named Leven's Gorge. The Sami might call this type of rapid geavnnis, meaning 'big rapids with falls in a large river (impossible or difficult to navigate in a boat)', or even borsi ('cauldron fall')[115] Whereas the English language lacks a rich vocabulary to describe different types of rapids or particular characteristics of deep and shallow water, such words abound in the Sami tongue. At one time the Picts may have had a similar breadth of terminology to describe the rapids and stiller waters on the Findhorn.

The many varieties of moving water.

Beyond Leven's Gorge, you come to a wood filled with giant European firs. Also known as the silver fir (abies alba), the species comes originally from the Alps and the Black Forest. In Europe they are widely used as Christmas trees. Their needles are particularly shiny, and they are a species that regenerates prolifically. These ones at Glenferness must have been planted at least a couple of centuries ago to reach such height and girth. To stand beneath such mammoth specimens creates a combined sense of humility, comfort and marvel. Their weighty presence makes me think of Christopher Stone's legal essay, Should Trees Have Standing.[116]

In the early 1970s in California, Walt Disney Enterprises was seeking to develop a wilderness area in the Sierra Nevada Mountains called Mineral King Valley. The Sierra Club brought a law suit against Disney for an injunction (interdict), claiming that the development would adversely affect the area's ecological and aesthetic balance. The court ruled that the Sierra Club had no 'standing' and could not seek, therefore, to block the development.

What Professor Stone sought to explore and convince the Californian courts was that natural objects, such as trees, rivers and mountains, deserve legal rights in the same way that companies have legal standing. As Professor Stone pointed out, because the natural world is not afforded its own rights, and instead the rights of a natural area's integrity lie with the proprietor, the legal options to protect an element of the natural world are limited. Instead, the only people that might via the court system seek to block an act that is damaging to the environment are those who have direct title and interest – in short, those with property rights.

Should Trees Have Standing explored the way in which a 'guardian' of a natural place – and not necessarily a proprietor, but someone with sufficient environmental knowledge – could legally represent an area, in much the same way that somebody be given power of attorney to represent a child or somebody that is incapax. At present in Europe and America, no such legal mechanism of environmental guardianship exists.

While some might consider the concept of the natural world having rights as being far fetched and impractical, it is no different from the time when women, children and many ethnicities were denied legal rights even within so-called modern democracies. Equally, corporations, universities and states require humans to advocate and act on their behalf. Indeed, the courts in Scotland have – perplexingly – gone so far as to allow companies human rights.[117] Professor Stone's argument continues to be debated and championed by those who believe that an 'Earth Jurisprudence' is the necessary legal progression to tackle the world's most significant environmental problems.

In Scotland, we have an extensive network of environmental laws established to protect the natural world. The majority of modern legislation has come from Brussels, and forms in my mind the single best thing to have come out of the European Union. Scotland is quite simply one of, if not the, most naturally stunning countries in the world. The Highlands and Islands in particular abound with such wildness and grandeur and light-dynamic character. In the trade-off world of politics where heavy corporate lobbying can justify in a politician's mind the merit in destroying wildlife and landscape in the name of fast money and 'jobs', the importance of the laws that exist and knowing your way around them is crucial.

Particularly rare and precious species and habitats find special protection from damage and disturbance under the European Birds and Habitats Directives. Add to this the European Water Framework Directive and its various trickle-down supporting pieces of legislation that raise the threshold on the quality of water that must be maintained (an 'ecological' quality at that), the likes of the Public Participation Directive which promotes greater community involvement, and the fact that the European Commission can be approached when your Member State is neglecting its duties, and you start to find that modern environmental justice is indeed a possibility. Mix in the Nature Conservation (Scotland) Act 2004, which mandates that all public bodies have to further the protection of biodiversity, and the fact that we have the Environmental Information (Scotland) Regulations 2004, which (akin to freedom of information legislation) allow far greater access for the public to previously unrecoverable documentation on the environment held by the likes of the government, and we have a pretty strong platform for insisting upon ecological protection.

The European Landscape Convention has only just been ratified, and it is thought that this will advance significantly the importance of and protection afforded to landscapes. We still, though, lack a Wilderness Act in Scotland, just as we lack a Wild Land Act. We also lack an equivalent to the Wild and Scenic Rivers Act which was introduced in the United States in 1968, essentially to safeguard the integrity of a range of American rivers from being developed. Scottish Natural Heritage (the government's advisors on wildlife and landscape matters) have begun exploring the notion of wild land as a policy matter, and will hopefully in due course push for appropriate legislation. The European Convention on Human Rights under Article 8 (right to private life) and Article 1/Protocol 1 (right to protection of property) creates another avenue for proprietors to seek the protection of the natural world, although as yet there is no express right to a healthy environment under this Convention.

Despite this breadth of environmental legislation, the two greatest barriers to environmental justice are cost and ignorance. In Scotland we have considerable scope for the public to state their case against a proposed development (which may result in an adverse impact to the built and natural environment) through the public inquiry system. Third parties have three basic options: to be considered 'relevant persons' and possibly instruct legal representation and expert witnesses; to appear at the inquiry to deliver a short statement; or to present a written submission. The problem, though, is cost. Public inquiries cost a serious amount of money, as do the likes of a Judicial Review challenging a government body's decision that you believe is incorrect. What tends to happen in the public inquiry system is that you have a disparity in representation with government and large companies able to instruct Advocates and numerous witnesses, while objectors can muster only a fraction of these resources.

For too long the modern world has proceeded on the basis that the irreversible exploitation of the environment is justified. Instead, such a position is misplaced and dysfunctional, and what is needed crucially is sound environmental education. With greater ecological understanding and consciousness, and greater honour for and cultural commitment to the natural world, we would have a far more self-regulating environmental protection system.

Beyond the wood of the European firs stands the Princess Stone. Around a thousand years ago when the Scandinavians sought to settle Moray, Prince Harald of Denmark was captured by King Fergus and imprisoned in the dungeons of Lochindorb Castle. Fergus's daughter, Princess Malvina, took a shine to the young Dane and secretly brought food to the dungeon. Well let's just say that Harald thought Malvina made a damn fine bowl of porridge, and pretty soon dungeon life on the island at Lochindorb became the stuff of dreams.

Unaware that both their fathers had arranged a marriage treaty for the two youngsters, they escaped across the loch before riding off across the Dava on a grey horse. When they reached the Findhorn at Dulsie the river was hurtling down in spate. Upon seeing a group of riders coming towards them and not realising that they were but the bearers of blessed tidings, Harald and Malvina attempted the impossible and tried to jump the river on horseback. In the tragedy that occurred, both the lovers and their horse drowned in the raging waters.[118] The cairn was erected in memory of them and astonishingly it was spared by the Great Floods of 1829 when the river formed an island around the stone monument.[119]

The path runs out not long after the Princess Stone and the riverbank is thick with alders. I'm not sure whether it would work with the species of alder we find in Scotland, but among the tribes of the First Nations peoples in British Columbia, the practice is to use alder chips (instead of oak as in Europe) for smoking salmon.

With Dulsie Bridge within striking distance and the late afternoon drawing on, I decide to make camp for the night. The grass is thick and bushy and will form a heavenly mattress for tonight's sleep. Today has been a longer day, and I must have been going for almost nine hours. The feet feel in good shape and there are no real blisters to cause concern. Taking off boots and socks and allowing my toes to comb their way into the grass is a simple luxury.

Having located a good rock for the stove, I go through the ritual of collecting water and firing up a brew of tea. This batch is going to be a sugary one – true builders' tea, or 'mountain brew' as a mountaineering teacher once passed on to me. Hot drinks are one of the most critical requirements for the body when out in the wilds. Himalayan climbers are known for saying that the secret of their success is hot fluids. The heavy dose of sugar serves to increase your electrolytes and aid balance. There's the calorie intake too that is so important, and we burn significantly more calories when playing and working away in the outdoors than is the case when office bound. Out here you can get away with eating the most outlandish mix of energy-packed food and still keep a slim figure. In the season when I was working as a ski instructor in the Alps and teaching mainly small kids (3 to 7 year olds) regularly for six hour-long blocks, a high energy breakfast was essential. In the Alps you find the best muesli available, and I went on a quest through the village's food stores to find the ultimate high octane breakfast. One of the secret ingredients was yoghurt drinks, which must have a higher density of calories per litre than any other drink. I then perfected my cereal mix of muesli, coco pops and sugar puffs, which, when combined with the yoghurt drink and a bread roll laced with Nutella spread, created a recipe for endurance.

It's a good idea to keep snacking in the outdoors too, and to graze your way throughout the day rather than sticking to three square meals. In North America people often refer to their stash of energy food as GORP – good ole raisins and peanuts. Add to this base some dried apple rings and apricots, smarties and pumpkin seeds, and it will keep your spirits up in difficult conditions for days. I shall never forget one moment on a ski-mountaineering trip in Chile when, having hauled sledges over miles of ice and rock in ski boots then pausing for breath, a friend handed round the finest Belgian toffees imaginable – one of those moments when you savour each chew and squish in your mouth of toffee juice, the rain coming down and the steam rising up from your jacket. At the end of a hard day in the outdoors – or at the end of a trip when you arrive back in civilisation – the basic things in life feel so much sweeter: a cool swim, a hot shower, a mug of fresh coffee, a bed, music, toast and butter, the voice of a loved one, a clean t-shirt.

The moon is rising
Through the birches
And the river is singing
A lullaby

CHAPTER FIVE

Wolves of the Dava Moor

'Scale of dragon, tooth of wolf
Witches' mummy'
Shakespeare, Macbeth iv.1.22

The first thing you notice upon reaching Dulsie Bridge is the big sky. After nearly two days of immersion in the forests of the lower Findhorn valley, I see the land now open up before me. Dulsie is the gateway to the section of river called the Streens. 'Streens' is a derivation of the Gaelic word 'scrian' meaning 'bridle', for the river threads its way through the plateau of the Dava Moor with the 'sinuous, narrow, supple and powerful' qualities of a bridle.[120]

Dulsie means 'The Knoll of the Fairies' and was named after the giant fairy hill of Shian Hillock on the right bank here. 'It was the rendezvous,' wrote George Bain, 'the metropolis, of all the fairy tribes up and down the Findhorn river.'[121] Fairy hills, or knowes, are the abodes of the original peoples of the Gaelic continuum, the Tuatha de Danaan, who fled underground and became the fairies when Ireland was invaded by the Milesians.[122] The fairy hill symbolises creativity. Legend has it that if you sleep the night on a fairy hill you will either receive the gift of art and music from the fairy folk, or else turn mad. Fairy hills also tend to demonstrate rich biological diversity, and it is safe to conclude that the fairy folk prefer natural beauty and abundance over ecological sterilisation.

The bridge at Dulsie was built as part of General Wade's old military road from Grantown-on-Spey to Fort George during the period of the Highland Clearances following the Jacobite defeat at Culloden in 1746. Once the bridge was built across the pool at Dulsie, the fairies began to disappear, 'betaking themselves in companies to places more remote'.[123]

If you were to follow the military road towards Grantown, you would come first of all to Aitnoch where there once lived the last in the line of minstrels of the River Findhorn. From Aitnoch if you were then to cut south-east over the hill, you would find yourself at the windswept Lochindorb.

Even though the loch lies out of sight from the River Findhorn, Lochindorb nevertheless sits within the river's watershed. The loch is drained by the River Dorback which then winds its way past stands of mature Scots pine underneath the Knock of Braemoray, before tumbling through Glenernie into the River Divie. In the middle of the loch lies the island fortress that became the home of the infamous Wolf of Badenoch.

Born Alexander Stewart, second son of Robert II, the Wolf was the Lord of Badenoch, the Earl of Buchan and Ross, and the Justiciar of Scotland North of the Forth. For years he battled against the church in Moray over landownership rights, culminating in his setting fire to the towns of Forres and Elgin, including the cathedral in Elgin, in the year 1390. 'Cruel, vindictive, despotic – a Celtic Attila'[124] is how one historian described the Wolf. Others have portrayed the figure as 'a good man'[125] and well respected by the Highlanders that followed him.

WOLVES OF THE DAVA MOOR

The Wolf would have proven a fascinating client to a medieval psychotherapist. Family dysfunction, the trappings of royalty, resentful of the church's increasing domination of temporal affairs throughout Scotland and Europe, susceptible to violent outbursts, yet choosing to live in one of Scotland's remoter corners, the Wolf must have been a complicated soul. We may never know the exact motives for the Wolf's campaign against the church. Maybe he felt a genuine sense of belonging and sought to protect the north from a form of centralised power with its roots in Europe. Perhaps he was driven by personal greed and insecurity with a desire simply to possess as much land as possible.

Back in the days when the Wolf made Lochindorb his home, the Dava would have looked very different. In those times the forest at Rothiemurchus stretched all the way across the Dava Moor to Cawdor. Scots pines would have been the principal species of tree in this old Caledonian forest, but there would also have been birch, willow, alder, aspen and rowan[126] This gigantic ancient forest known as Leanach which 'embraced the Monadhliath range and its foot-hills'[127] was still in existence at the beginning of the 18th century. Sir Thomas Dick Lauder recounted the reports of a man from Aviemore who declared that: 'When I was a youth, I used to go in underneath the shade of the forest on this side of the woods of Dulnan [River Dulnain], and I hardly ever saw the sun again till I got out of it below Cawdor Castle'.[128]

Many people today consider that rural Scotland has always consisted predominantly of heather moorland, which is not the case. Ratcliffe and McVean demonstrated that forest interspersed with savannah once stretched across Scotland from coast to coast covering an area of around 1.5 million hectares.[129]

I recall one scientist interpreting this position by saying that it would have been hypothetically possible for a red squirrel to travel in an unbroken treetop journey from Aberdeen to Kyle of Lochalsh (at the present time, as it happens, there are in fact no red squirrels living in North West Scotland). Open space between the trees is likely to have been the pattern thereby allowing grazing animals such as aurochs to roam, rather than the simpler idea of there having been solid forest across the land.[130] Extensive illegal logging of the forests across the Dava between the years of 1566 and 1573 prompted Mary Queen of Scots to write a letter in 1566 decrying their destruction.[131] Today only 1.1% of the original, native Caledonian forest in Scotland remains.[132]

'Ugly' is the word Thomas Henderson chose to describe the Dava in its present form.[133] It's not the word I would choose, as I consider the moor to form such an exceptional expanse of wildness and light.

> Clouds of silver rainlight
> Gathering at the gates
> Of the Streens
> For a chase
> Down the river canyons
> To the sea
>
> Aurora borealis
> On a late autumn night
> Sky dome above the ridges
> Fiery green and white

WOLVES OF THE DAVA MOOR

Early morning
Apricot glow
Spreading Westwards
From Ben Rinnes

But the Dava seems lifeless. Yes, there are grouse which provide sport to estates, and you may see wild goats and the occasional owl or hen harrier. However, there could be so much more life here. The area could be far healthier. Were the trees to return – as they have started to appear in some pockets through planting and natural regeneration – then so too would a greater diversity of wildlife. Like blood circulating through a body, once again bringing colour and movement.

The task of replanting expanses such as the wider Dava area (by which I mean the watersheds of the Rivers Nairn, Findhorn, Lossie and Spey) with native tree species is far from impossible. All it needs is a helping hand from the species that knocked it cold in the first place. You only need to look at the stalwart work of volunteer groups such as Trees for Life that have been replanting the ancient forests in Glen Affric to see what a difference can be made when there is dedication to habitat restoration. This type of work needs greater support, however, if we are to reforest more of Scotland. In order to tackle the challenge most effectively, I believe we need an 'Earth Corps' as based upon the model of Franklin D. Roosevelt's Civilian Conservation Corps (CCC).[134] During the Great Depression in the United States, the CCC created 44 wildlife refuges, planted 2 billion trees, and employed 3 million Americans. The late American mountaineer and conservationist David Brower described how having a job in which you were able to camp in the woods, repair overgrazed stream banks, replant the prairies with trees, sleep around a campfire under a full moon, and listen to goose music as you worked to save geese populations, would have provided a high quality of life to those involved in such a venture.[135]

Although the principal focus for British and American governments in recent years has been to 'rid the world of terror', what is now finally being acknowledged at a political level is that the greatest threat to human survival is climate change.[136] Climate change is predicted to threaten life on Earth in a variety of ways. The melting of the ice sheets is something that is being seen as a major problem. Sea levels are anticipated to rise and there is a danger that communities currently just above sea level could be flooded. Diseases such as malaria are also predicted to spread worldwide as disease-carrying mosquitoes are able to move further towards the poles. Extreme weather, too, in the form of hurricanes and blizzards is forecast to increase. Furthermore, the Gulf Stream's action of pumping warm currents around the North Atlantic will slow if not cease given the predicted lack of salinity in Arctic waters as a result of melting ice, and the result could be that northerly countries such as Scotland will experience winter climate conditions similar to those of Siberia and Labrador.

Given the environmental service that trees provide in off-setting carbon, I believe we should be engaged in a far more comprehensive reforestation programme throughout the UK. To this extent, we could be channelling significant military efforts towards reforesting the planet. It would be peace-making rather peace-keeping. We needn't stop short of military involvement either – reforestation could provide countless jobs to the unemployed and engage young people for a stint in the outdoors after school. Furthermore, as David Brower suggested in Let the Mountains Talk, Let the Rivers Run, highly skilled professionals might also be tempted to take sabbaticals so that they could participate in such a programme. How many hydraulic engineers, asked Brower, would prefer to spend time restoring rivers rather than constructing giant dams? How many biologists would jump at the chance to spend time in the outdoors instead of being cooped up in a laboratory? How many business studies graduates would derive satisfaction from assessing the costs of failing to protect the planet?[137]

Treaties such as the Kyoto Protocol are essential in encouraging cohesive international efforts to tackle climate change. However, signatures and rhetoric need to be followed up in practice. We need effective action instead of activity, and commitment instead of procrastination.

As for the costs: well there are always charity donations, but the urgency, seriousness and scale of the problem dwarfs charity. Businesses keen to become 'carbon neutral' could (and in a growing number of cases do) certainly contribute to tree-planting programmes, but why aren't we devoting military expenditure to this kind of thing? When you think of the billions of pounds of taxpayers' money that are frittered away needlessly each year on the obsolete need for nuclear weapons, I for one would be far happier paying my taxes if I knew that some of it was to be spent on tree and habitat restoration.

Were it my decision on how the government should spend money on stimulating initiatives to tackle climate change, I would strongly recommend that the annual allocation of around £1 billion in the UK that currently goes mainly to wind power generation companies be reconsidered. The Renewables Obligation Certificate (ROC) scheme is a mechanism whereby every power generating company that provides a stipulated percentage of its energy by renewable sources (wind, hydro, biomass and tidal) receives monetary incentives from the government. Those companies that fail to meet the target can either pay a fine, or can purchase credits from other companies that have provided a level of their energy output in excess of the prescribed amount.

On the one hand, the scheme has woken the business sector up to the issue of climate change, and in this it has served a much-needed purpose. However, there are four strategic problems with the UK government's position. Firstly, there is no government strategy as to the optimal mix of forms of renewable energy. As a result, the majority of commercial initiatives that have run after ROC funds have opted for on-shore wind power – arguably the most straightforward form of industrial-scale renewable energy production in terms of available technology and the corresponding investment required.

Secondly, with the proliferation of wind farm applications that have arisen amidst this Klondike-like rush for fortune, there is still no national strategy illustrating the most appropriate locations for on-shore wind power. A strategy might consider factors such as wind speeds and proximity to transmission balanced against landscape and visual impacts; adverse impacts upon protected species (in particular raptors and migratory species protected under the EU Birds Directive and the Wildlife & Countryside Act 1981) and habitats (such as blanket bog – one of the most important carbon 'sinks' on the planet along with forests and coral reefs which all play the ecological role of absorbing and storing carbon dioxide); as well as biodiversity, noise, tourism, hydrology and planning policy.

Thirdly, there seems little logic or efficiency in seeking to transmit relatively intermittent power (the average output of wind farms is around only 30% of generation capacity) created in remote, unspoilt, non-industrialised, low-populated areas across Scotland to the centres of demand in the south – when arguably it would be more efficient and less of a blight to line the estuaries and ports of the Clyde, Forth, Mersey, Wirral, Severn and Thames with turbines (for example, as you find in Rotterdam).

Fourthly, the technological fix of operating white turbines on remote hillsides is not the panacea for combating climate change – our change must go far further than simply renewable energy production, so as to initiate greater energy efficiency in terms of housing insulation and transport as well as to restore carbon sinks in the form of forests. In short, whilst the ROC scheme has led to major changes in business attitudes towards the commercial opportunities created by climate change, a significant proportion of these funds should be directed instead to wide scale tree-planting schemes and energy efficiency initiatives.

From Dulsie Bridge I make a recce of the pool at Dulsie as preparation for the canoe journey back downriver. The rapid that runs into the bridge pool is grade 4 whitewater and will be a real challenge in an open canoe. I want to see my options for coming ashore above the rapid. There is a spot around the corner where I should be able to catch an eddy, and then exit up a grass bank. I then decide to retrace my steps back to the bridge and cross over to the Cawdor side of the river. In order to cover the 16 miles or so upriver to Tomatin by nightfall, I figure that the road up to Drynachan will allow me to cover ground more quickly than the river bank path. Although this means that I won't be right beside the river for a few miles, I'll have the chance to explore the section by canoe.

WHITE RIVER

For the first couple of miles the road passes through birch woods and in the cool breeze of the early morning it is difficult to tell whether the trees are still asleep or just plain laid back. Birch appears at the centre of many cultures across the Arctic/ sub-Arctic band. Among tribes in Siberia, birch is called the 'Girl of the Forest' for its blond autumn tresses.

> A pastiche
> Of sheep shit
> And wool
> Decorates the road
>
> A woodcock
> Carries her chick
> Kangaroo-style
> From ditch
> To marsh reeds
>
> Forest gaps
> Reveal
> The distant knuckles
> Of Ben Avon

After the farm at Banchor the road sweeps down to river level and the terrain feels alpine. Curlew surf the low ground. Gulls circle the alders. Peewits journey upstream along the 'bird path'. This concept of the 'bird path' is something that Kenneth White has explored and expounded in a number of his works. To 'tread the bird path' is a Zen Buddhist concept that means giving up attachments and moving freely through the world. White has also described the phenomenon of the 'sky road' in certain shamanic ceremonies of the Altai where a line of birch trees is surmounted by bird images.[138] So we have this fusion of natural bird flight, freedom from the confines of the ego, and a shamanic birch tree launch-pad into the farther realms of consciousness.

Simply watching a bird's trajectory can trip you into a field of aliveness.

> The turn
> The glide
> The jink
> The dip
> The ecstatic
> Purity of line

Old Scots pines drilled by the beaks of woodpeckers create a gateway to Carnoch. The air is filled with the sap-like smell of broom. Rabbits go about their work. Larch and pines cloak the steep banks of the Carnoch Burn. Until about a century ago at Carnoch ('The Field of the Cairn'), the old ceremony of deasil used to take place in which men and horses would circle the cairn three times in a sunwise direction to bring good luck.

Passing the shooting lodge of Cawdor Estate at Drynachan, one of the keepers who work here pulls up in his Landrover to check where I'm heading. I tell him I'm walking up to Tomatin. The keeper kindly describes the best path to take to reach Shenachie so that I don't disturb any grouse chicks. From the far side of the Landrover cab beams the most incredibly charismatic, mutley-toothed smile of his dog – what seems to be a Jack Russell/Cairn terrier cross. As the vehicle pulls away the sound of water tumbling over the rocks in the Drynachan Burn rumbles down the creek and under a bridge. A little further on stands the startling sight of a bright orange bothy, the colour of an oyster catcher's beak.

Over the crest of the hill past Daless, I rest and look out upon the foothills of the Monadhliath Mountains. Two days ago, the mountains seemed a long way off. By tomorrow afternoon I should be in the heart of the Monadhliaths.

A cliff the colour of salmon flesh pillars the hill from the river. On the far bank sits the farm of Quilichan. Cuckoos call. A current of warm air slips over the heather.

Wild flowers abound here at this time of year. This would seem a direct result of the absence of sheep, which were removed from the majority of the hill ground at Cawdor Estate in the mid 1990s. Yet whereas I thought that sheep were the scourge of biodiversity in the Highlands, having spoken to a number of sheep farmers I have come to see another angle. Sheep can in fact play a positive role in allowing flora to grow. After the early flowers, sheep can help keep longer grasses from choking more fragile plants. Indeed, grazing livestock on high ground and woodland has long been an integral part of Highland agricultural life, and a natural mimic to auroch, wild white cattle and wild boar that became extinct.[139] Summer grazing traditionally took place in the Highlands through the sheiling system, where livestock would be driven in May to summer pastures and then return to lower ground after the harvest[140] and carrying capacity was controlled through the process of 'souming' in which a tenant would be entitled to graze a stipulated number of animals.[141]

Sheep grazing can contribute positively to enhancing biodiversity on high ground and in woodlands. However, there has been widespread abuse from a mixture of too many sheep being allowed on the ground and a decline in active, sound shepherding practices. Sheep farming began in the region in the 1760s when the Highlands switched from a cattle to a sheep economy. In the 19th century there was a boom in sheep prices and, correspondingly, many tenants were cleared from the interior so that estates could raise more sheep. Following the extermination of the wolf in the Scottish Highlands in the mid-18th century, the ceiling on the number of livestock that could be kept on the ground was effectively lifted. If you combine unrestricted numbers with the fact that sheep tend to graze hill ground more closely and destructively than cattle, the result is an unsustainable exploitation of the land.[142]

Part of today's problem is that sheep prices have plummeted compared to what they once were, and employing dedicated shepherds is economically unviable in most places. Interestingly, however, shepherding is currently seeing a renaissance on grouse moors where the link between well-managed flocks and abundant grouse numbers is being proven, and where the costs of shepherding can be absorbed within the financial context of grouse revenue. A number of estates throughout the River Findhorn watershed as well as in Aberdeenshire and the Borders are practising a method of dipping and 'spotting' sheep regularly throughout the non-winter months when the sheep are up on the high ground, and then moving flocks around grouse moors to tick-infested 'hotspots' and to areas that have not been overgrazed. Purists may argue that a grouse moor is an intensely managed environment and that it is dangerous to talk of supporting biodiversity in this frame. Nevertheless, grouse moors and gamekeeping form a cultural and economic cornerstone of the watershed, and this delicately, ever-fluctuating balance between sheep, grouse and wildlife is something that deserves fuller study and attention.[143]

WHITE RIVER

Mountain speedwell
Spreads its blue
Throughout the grasses

Finches balance
On the bracken tips

A snowfall
Of cotton
Bobs on the haugh

In the past, funerals in the Streens consisted of the mourners carrying the coffin along the track upriver to the churchyard at Moy. This part of the Streens is impassable to vehicles and the inhabitants saw this tradition as 'a sacred duty' whatever the weather.[144]

Steep interlocking spurs gripped by birch squeeze the river into its narrowest channel in this section at the Pass of Pollochaig ('Pool of the Little Black One'). The pass here has not always been the outlet for the river. Geological investigations have proven that a great loch used to exist here during a 'remote geological period'. The pass, it is thought, was blocked off either by ice debris or by the solid rock of the cliff at Pollochaig. Fertile haughs and water terrace marks throughout the valley of Strathdearn indicate the extent of this loch. So at one time, the River Findhorn made a detour through Loch Moy, flowing into the valley of the River Nairn.[145]

Many years ago the Laird of Pollochaig, 'Black' John MacQueen, incurred the anger of the fairies of the area by giving away a set of magic fairy candles to a friend. The candles had been given to

MacQueen as a present from the fairies of Strathdearn so that he might enter into the realms where the fairy folk held their merrymakings[146] There was, however, a condition attached to the gift in that he should never part with the candles to anybody.

When Ian McAngus MacGillivray of Dunmaglass reported that his wife had been carried off by the fairy folk to Tomshangen ('The Hill of the Ants'), MacGillivray's laird, Captain Ban, told him that fairy candles were the essential kit they would need for staging such a rescue mission. A messenger was then despatched to Black John MacQueen requesting the loan of the magic candles of Pollochaig.

Black John obliged with the request and handed over one of the candles to the messenger, urging him on the strictest terms, however, not to turn around on his ride back to Dunmaglass. Spooked on the return journey by the mysterious sounds of horses' hooves and carriage wheels, the first rider succumbed to turning around and at once the candle disappeared from his hand. The fairies had nabbed it.

A second messenger was then sent to Black John MacQueen to ask for a spare. MacQueen, in true neighbourly spirit, thought nothing of it and parted with a second candle, again warning the messenger never to turn around until he reached his final destination. The messenger managed to reach Farr before a cacophony of high-pitched fairy screeching drew him to turn around. Two-nil to the fairies.

When a third messenger arrived at Pollochaig, Black John MacQueen seemed little surprised as he knew just how determined a rider must be not to give in to the tricks of the fairy folk. As well as handing over another magic candle, MacQueen provided the messenger with a large black stone and advised him to return via a different route that involved fording the River

Findhorn. The river was in spate and it would have been curtains had he attempted a crossing. At Black John's suggestion, the messenger hurled the black stone across the torrent to the far bank and, lo and behold, found himself across on the other side. The fairies, who did not like to cross the river, were outplayed and the candle was delivered to MacGillivray at Dunmaglass.

MacGillivray and his laird, Captain Ban, then set off to Tomshangen Hill and upon arriving there lit the magic candle. A little door appeared from behind which came the sound of dancing and celebration. They entered the hill without knocking to find Mrs MacGillivray dancing reels with the fairies. Mrs MacGillivray was baffled when her husband told her that she had been missing for a year and a day, as she was convinced she had only been gone since the previous night.

The fairies rushed at the two men but the light from the candle acted as a barrier. As soon as the MacGillivrays and Captain Ban got outside the hillock, the door slammed with a bang. The inside of Tomshangen, the Ants' Hill, was never to be seen again by human eyes. As the story goes, Black John MacQueen suffered financially for the loyalty he showed to his friends by offending the fairies.

The wind picks up. The track leaves Nairnshire and enters Inverness-shire. Cawdor passes into Moy. The terrain feels rougher now as the way passes over rocks instead of grass. The river is narrow here. The landscape austere. The sky stretched taut between the mountain tops. This is northern land. It could be Alaska, and a moose would not seem out of place.

Up ahead two fishermen cast into the pool at Pollochaig from the far bank. As I draw level, we talk for a short while. 'Nothing moving – haven't seen a fish all day,' they tell me across the current. They explain that they started about a mile upstream this morning and have gradually worked their way down river. They have come up from Ayrshire for the week. This is their first time fishing the River Findhorn. I tell them about the gorge and the forests downstream.

I then come to a lagoon that must have been abandoned by the river during the course of recent spates. The water is clear and filled with tadpoles. The sand surrounding the lagoon makes an ideal spot to rest and take a late lunch. Rummaging through the pack for some sustenance, I pull out a can of sardines, a stack of crackers and some dried apricots – a combination I would never consider eating at home, but in the outdoors when you are hungry such flavours can form a banquet.

I suppose the ultimate way to eat on a journey such as this would be to hunt and gather as you go. When the Picts moved up river in the spring they would have caught fish as they travelled inland. For indigenous cultures throughout the world that still follow a hunter-gatherer existence, the search for food forms the principal focus of the day. When you consider animals too, their priorities are clear – food, shelter and reproduction. Civilisation seems to have drawn our attention away from these fundamentals of survival on Earth. Instead, we humans can become preoccupied with the most trivial of issues – is the car clean, is the grass cut, has the soufflé risen ... The outdoors provide us with the opportunity to shed these unnecessary worries and focus on what really matters. It's not life threatening if the colours of your clothes clash, if you don't shave, if you can't check your emails, if you smell like a goat, if you don't read a newspaper. Instead you can focus on fresh air and exercise, food, fluids, sleep and witnessing the planet's grandeur and intricacies.

WHITE RIVER

If I was a purist, I would be out fishing on the river for my lunch (well, that would technically be poaching). There would be no guarantee that I would catch a fish, and so I might go hungry. I would have to sit and wait until I was successful before having the energy to move on. It could, therefore, take weeks to travel the river in this way, but that would no doubt bring me closer to my surroundings. In the modern world we manage to short cut the need to hunt and gather by pushing a trolley around a supermarket. We say that time is saved, only to fill that time with other sometimes non-essential demands. The more time we save from not having to gather food (let alone cook) or not sleeping a full night's sleep so that we can meet that deadline, the faster our lives become.

So I have not brought a fishing rod (although have done so on canoeing and sea-kayaking trips) and have stocked up on food to sustain me along the way. For a number of years I was vegetarian, which in the outdoors is a cinch as you don't need to worry about meat going bad. Then I found that on longer mountaineering trips I would start to hallucinate about steaks. Not chocolate cake, not tofu, not even pizza, but steak. It must have been my body crying out for protein. Today's lunchtime main course of sardines hits the spot. Opening a can of sardines is a quick and simple way to fish, albeit without the grace of fly fishing.

By the time I start off again, the two fishermen have packed up and are heading upstream to the bucket bridge at Shenachie. Laden with fishing equipment, the two figures walk slowly through the long grass. As they move out of sight, the pool beside the rocky moraine where they were fishing starts to come alive with rising trout.

On the far side of the haugh at Shenachie two other figures stoke a bonfire. As I reach the fire, the two gamekeepers have stopped for a break while the fire burns down. They are burning rotten planks from a disused bothy. Even though I am warm from the walk, it still feels good to be standing by a fire. The fire is about four feet across in diameter. I can feel the skin on my hands tighten in the heat.

We start chatting away about the fire and the weather. I introduce myself. 'We heard you were coming,' they tell me. 'We were at Margaret's the other day when you phoned her.' I had indeed phoned Margaret at Ruthven some four days ago to find out the best route up through Shenachie. Bush telegraph at its finest.

An osprey spirals the air currents
Searching for fishing holes

Looking back onto the steep hillside on the left bank at Shenachie, the conversation drifts onto the subject of the last wolf in Scotland, which was killed around here back in 1743. The keepers point to some of the ruined foundations across the haugh where MacQueen of Pollochaig (a relation of Black John) would have lived. In those days a number of families lived in crofts at Pollochaig and Shenachie, keeping small numbers of livestock, growing oats, cutting peats, while at the same time working for the estate at Moy. So when the Laird of Mackintosh at Moy summoned the estate workers to gather before embarking on a wolf hunt, MacQueen was one the people expected to pitch up.

As it turned out on that morning when everyone had gathered at Moy Hall, MacQueen did not show for an hour. By the time he arrived the Laird was close to exploding with temper. 'I am little used to wait thus for any man,' stormed Mackintosh, 'and still less for thee, Pollochock, especially when such game is afoot as we are boon after!'[147] MacQueen acted obliviously, leading Mackintosh to believe that he had not received any news about the wolf hunt. Just at the point when the Laird was about to have a hernia with frustration, MacQueen reached inside the folds of his plaid and produced the head of the wolf they were seeking. In return for his deed MacQueen was gifted the ground at Shenachie. Since that morning no wolves have run in the mountains and forests of Scotland.

Lying in the grass gazing up onto the mountain ridges around Shenachie, I think of Aldo Leopold's goose-bumpingly powerful essay on the importance of wolves from A Sand County Almanac [148] and how ultimately it is the only that mountain that 'has lived long enough to listen objectively to the howl of a wolf.' In the essay, Leopold described the experience that proved the crossroads in his work and writing as an ecologist, a turning point when he saw for the first time that managing the natural environment solely as a resource for humans is doomed, and that it is essential for humans to begin thinking about the natural world in deeper, more ecological ways and relationships. Leopold, who was working for the United States Forest Service in Arizona and New Mexico at the time, chanced upon a pack of wolves. Never one to pass up the chance to shoot a wolf, particularly because as he then thought 'fewer wolves meant more deer, that no wolves would mean a hunters' paradise', Leopold shot and killed a mother wolf. Approaching the fallen wolf, Leopold watched 'a fierce green fire die in her eyes'.[149] That was the moment when he realised that his theory of exterminating wolves to boost deer was both shallow and misguided. Without wolves, as Leopold explained, natural control on deer numbers is removed. In turn, all edible bushes and saplings are browsed 'first to an anaemic desuetude, and then to death'. In the end, it is the deer that face starvation. This ecological consequence chimes with the words of the factor to the Earl of Moray in 1707 when he exclaimed to his employer 'no woods, no deir'.[150]

Aldo Leopold's story describes so succinctly the ecological necessity of having large predators such as wolves in an ecosystem. In particular, the wolf provides a mechanism of 'negative feedback' by controlling prey populations.[151] Without the effect of wolves 'trimming the herd to fit the range'.[152] red deer numbers have spiralled out of control to figures that far exceed the carrying capacity.[153] The result in Scotland has been what Sir Frank Fraser Darling once described as 'a wet desert'.[154] Not only do wolves play the role of minimising the destruction of trees and flora, but they also supply food for scavengers.[155] In short, wolves are an essential component in forest and mountain habitats throughout the sub-Arctic region, and without their presence native ecosystems degenerate.

Considering the importance and urgency for reforestation throughout the UK – not just as a prevention to the ramifications of climate change, but also to improve freshwater habitats for salmon – how is it that over 260 years have elapsed since the last wolf was killed in Scotland and we haven't yet managed to reintroduce even a small number of wolves into the Scottish wilds? The two major reasons, it would seem, are the threat to livestock and humans' fear of wolves.

The livestock rancher versus environmentalist debate is an old, well-worn battle. Be it snow leopards in Pakistan and Ladakh, cheetahs in Namibia, tigers in India, or pumas in Chile, the argument between farmers wanting to protect their economic interests and conservationists seeking to protect wild species continues across the globe. The successful reintroduction of wolves to Yellowstone National Park in Wyoming has been one such example of contention in the 'Wild West'.[156] But there are compromises that can be made with farmers, such as compensation for any livestock killed by wolves, as is practised in Spain.[157] If the government was genuinely serious about adopting measures to counteract climate change then such a fund – even if it did run at a couple of million pounds per year, such as at Yellowstone, and included funding to cover radio collaring, telemetry and education as well as livestock loss – would be but negligible, compared to the potentially trillions of pounds worth of damage that climate change, if not tackled, is predicted to cause. Surely this forms part of a sound insurance policy.

The second reason why people seem to show resistance to wolf reintroduction is fear. For the record, in North America there is no scientifically acceptable evidence available to support the claim that wild wolves are dangerous to humans.[158] Indeed, reports of wolf attacks on humans throughout Asia and Europe are few and far between.[159] In Sweden, the gamekeeping superintendent for the Swedish Crown Forests stated that he could not find 'a single authenticated case of a wolf attacking a human in Europe in the past 150 years'.[160] Certainly the childhood fairy stories and folk tales of the European tradition such as Little Red Riding Hood and The Three Little Pigs instil an image in our minds of wolves being evil, malicious creatures. In truth, wolves are generally shy of humans and try to avoid us as much as possible.[161] Just as Jaws falsely portrayed Great White sharks as being intent on killing humans, so too have folk tales perpetuated similar illusions about wolves.

This irrational fear may have deeper roots than simply fear of physical attack. Wolves, it may be argued, symbolise a 'shadow side' in the natural world. The inability of humans to fully understand and control the behaviour of these enigmatic, elusive creatures furthers a mystery and darkness that preoccupies our perceptions. Similarly, by trying to eradicate wolves it is as if humans do not want to see 'the way of all flesh'. As discussed above, there are ecological dangers caused by removing predators such as wolves from the equation. There are also psychological dangers, as Carl Jung pointed out.

Jung pioneered the idea that a 'shadow side' forms an inseparable part of our psyches and is the counterpart to our conscious ego. It is in this shadow that the parts of our psyche that have been repressed, rejected or denied may be found. [162]

Wild creatures symbolically provide a warning sign to humans – a healthy reminder – that we ignore this side of our nature at our peril. Engaging with the 'wild', shadow side of our beings can help unlock and stimulate a reservoir of creative potential. On this point, the psychotherapist Howard Clinebell commented that this inner dimension in 'many 'civilised' people... is deeply repressed.' [163]

This point of Clinebell's is echoed by the philosopher David Abram in his outstanding book The Spell of the Sensuous[164] when he commented on the evolution of the human body 'in delicate reciprocity with the manifold textures, sounds and shapes of an animate earth'. In Abram's view, failing to engage with the wild was 'to rob our own senses of their integrity, and to rob our own minds of their coherence.'

Nevertheless, looking into this shadow can be painful and

something that requires honesty if the process is to prove effective. Part of the reason why humans fear looking into the 'shadow' of the wolf may be explained by the fact that a wolf is considered to take your stare and then turn it back at you. As the Bella Coola Indians of North West Canada believed, there was once somebody who attempted to change all the animals of the world into men, but only managed to make human the eyes of the wolf.[165] Facing up to wild animals requires facing up to our innermost selves.

In the meantime, Great Britain remains clouded by the double standards and hypocrisy of expecting other nations throughout the world to protect tigers and sharks and polar bears and gorillas, yet we are not prepared to follow suit. What is more, we blatantly choose to ignore international environmental laws and treaties that we are party to, such as the Bern Convention on the Conservation of European Wildlife and Natural Habitats and the European Habitats Directive, which require member/signatory countries to investigate the feasibility of reintroducing native species. Yet people are captivated by wildlife documentaries on National Geographic Channel and by the likes of Sir David Attenborough. It would seem that we seek the experience of wild nature from the safety of our living rooms, and not the real deal. As Aldo Leopold warned, too much safety can lead to danger in the long run.[166]

Reintroducing wolves to Scotland is no trivial step, and community education as well as consultation and mediation with farmers and estates would be crucial for any successful wide scale project to take place. However, a recent scientific paper that appeared in the Proceedings of the Royal Society entitled 'Wolf Reintroduction to Scotland: Public Attitudes and Consequences for Red Deer Management' concluded that the Scottish public has a generally positive view of species reintroduction.[167] Farmers tend to be the exception to this acceptance, although the study found that farmers were far less negative than their representative bodies.

Let us also not underestimate the need for reforestation across Scotland and for vitally functioning ecological systems. A major appraisal and design of the way in which we live needs to be addressed if we are to find a means of living sustainably in synch with the rhythms of the natural world. If we are serious about our survival on this planet, we need to start laying the groundwork for wildlife reintroduction and indigenous reforestation projects to be put into practice. Wolves can teach us the humility we need to remember that we humans are not the masters of the universe, but part of something far greater than just humanity. Adopting these changes is not about doom and depression, but rather it is about healing and restoration. Wolves can help us to rediscover that sense of intense aliveness, that sap of vitality, that call of the wild.

The path upriver from Shenachie hugs the river bank, winding its way through blaeberries and mature silver birch trees. Across the river stand hundreds of tree shelters protecting native hardwoods that have been planted by Moy Estate. Junipers patch the hillside.

Ten oyster catchers wing their way in formation over the rapids. At every new section of the river I come to there is always an oyster catcher guiding the way. You could say they are the hosts of the river.

As the river straightens, the valley of Strathdearn opens up and in the distance lie the Monadhliaths. It seems strange to think that I am only about half way up the river at this point, because Tomatin is now so close. Until now, I've always tended to associate Tomatin with the headwaters of the river. It's another good two days from here on foot (with a pack) to reach the source, but arriving in Strathdearn feels like something of a landmark. It is a different zone from the Dava, and from the forests, the coastal plain and the shore.

At one time there used to be 'eleven smokes' between Shenachie and Ruthven on the left bank of the river. Many people may have left the area, but Margaret and her family remain at Ruthven. When I called Margaret a few days back to ask her advice on how best to travel through the Streens, she suggested I drop in for a cup of tea on my way up to Tomatin. It is an offer too kind to turn down.

I enter the garden gate and am welcomed at the door by her dogs. Margaret shows me in to the sitting room and I take a seat by the fire. It feels so good to remove the pack and take the weight off my feet. Margaret, who is in her late eighties, offers me tea and biscuits and I can wholeheartedly say that it is one of the best cups of tea I have ever had in my life. She tells me that Alan, her son, is working up at Coignafearn at the moment but that I should bump into him up there tomorrow. We then talk about salmon fishing and the river.

Margaret's generosity reminds me of the ways in Ladakh on the Tibetan Plateau and the Berber villages in the Atlas Mountains where travellers are often welcomed by the locals of a village and fed and watered. Then later, the host would ask some questions such as where the traveller has come from, where they are heading, what they saw and such like. This age-old custom can also be found in the epic tales of writers such as Homer and Tolkien. It is that order of providing the traveller with sustenance and then asking questions which demonstrates a deep level of equanimity, trust and openness in the host.

104

In Ladakh you would be offered butter tea and apricots. In Morocco it is peppermint tea. In Patagonia there is yerba maté. In Scotland we offer tea, and foreigners who come and visit (particularly from America) always seemed astonished at the amount of tea drunk throughout the day. There is power in a hot drink. Like fire, hot fluids focus attention, revive spirits and can draw a group back together again.

It is now late afternoon and I need to press on upstream. As I wave goodbye to Margaret, I say that I hope she and Alan will come and visit downriver sometime soon. Even though we live over 30 miles apart in different terrain, being from the same river makes us part of the same community.

CHAPTER SIX

Stags of Strathdearn

'One of these light clouds, which we were watching, was suddenly caught in an eddy of wind, and, after being twisted into strange fantastic shapes, was lifted from the face of the mountain like a curtain, leaving in its place a magnificent stag, of a size of body and stretch of antler rarely seen; he was not above three hundred yards from us, and standing in full relief between us and the sky. After gazing around him, and looking like the spirit of the mountain, he walked slowly on towards a ridge which connected two shoulders of the mountain together.'

Charles St. John,
Wild Sports and Natural History of the Highlands [168]

In the wide-open country of Strathdearn, landmarks appear closer than they are. But half an hour on from Ruthven, and Tomatin still seems distant. Perhaps it's just an early evening mirage. A few more bends in the river and I should be there. Tracking a way up the flood plain, the gulls screech overhead – any non-gull species does not have a hope in hell of entering Tomatin without the gull alarm being raised.

A fisherman casts into the current from the far bank at

Corrybrough. He is an elderly man. We start talking across the pool. He asks if I've seen anyone fishing on my travels. I tell him about the two near Shenachie. He hasn't caught anything so far today, but his son landed an eight pound salmon two days ago.

A brace of wigeon swing up around the bend. The male makes its characteristic whistling sound, flashing its white wing patches as it passes. The female is a brownish colour. Wigeon are smaller and more compact than mallard. We watch them as they rotate the lead position, weaving their way out of sight.

After a network of grassy fields, you come to the giant viaducts at Tomatin. First towers the road bridge of the A9 overhead, then upstream stands the railway bridge. The work that must have gone into such mammoth constructions is staggering, especially the work on the railway bridge in the pre-crane days. The technical excellence of the railway bridge – like so many old railway bridges throughout the country – is astonishing. What I find even more impressive is the way in which such a giant structure fits in with the landscape without detracting from the beauty of the surroundings. I suspect that the designers many years ago must have paid great attention to the character of the place in order to make the bridge fit with the landscape. The result being natural and built environments merging together in a complementary manner.

The river is strewn with rocks around here, so much so that canoeists seldom paddle the river upstream of Tomatin. The third bridge – the bridge that carries the road out of Tomatin itself, and which was a 1926 replacement of Thomas Telford's 1833 design – provides a view of the river groynes which were the subject of some controversy in the late 1990s.

The idea behind such groynes is that they help to vary the speed of water through a pool, and so improve the habitat, attracting more salmon to a certain spot. Although they are a relatively rare sight on the River Findhorn, groynes have become increasingly common on wider rivers such as the Ness, Spey and Tay. In many cases, a well-positioned boulder or groyne can help improve the fishing in a pool, although it all depends on how the work is carried out. On some rivers this practice has been taken to extremes with river beds excavated and unsettled. Whereas the fishing may improve in the short term, the next spate can undo all the work, choking downstream pools with silt and gravel. Under the Water Environment (Controlled Activities) (Scotland) Regulations 2005 that form part of the European Water Framework Directive, any alteration in hydrology through human activity is now closely monitored.

What about other human developments in the natural world, such as dams, Sitka plantations, transmission pylons, GM crops, and now wind farms? How appropriate and sustainable are each of these individual projects and larger plans? Will a development blend into the landscape seamlessly? Will it respect its surroundings? Will it be compatible with the ecological integrity of the place? Will it have style?

A timeless rule which I believe can be applied to virtually any development to test whether or not it will adversely impact upon the natural world is 'The Land Ethic' of Aldo Leopold. 'A thing is right,' declared Leopold, 'when it tends to preserve the integrity, stability, and beauty of the biotic community. It is wrong when it tends otherwise.'[169] The most widely applied test in Europe for sustainable development is the United Nations Brundtland Report of 1987, which addresses intergenerational equity – essentially not doing anything that might compromise the wellbeing of future generations. Leopold's sustainablility test, however, is more ecologically focussed, and requires us to look at our direct relationship with the Earth. I'm of the view that Leopold's approach offers more direction than the Brundtland Report test. If we look after the Earth and treat it with respect, we shall pass on a worthy legacy to future generations. In ancient Celtic culture (and indeed in a number of indigenous cultures today) there was a principle of thinking seven generations ahead before doing anything with the land. Ancient wisdom that deserves consideration at every single planning inquiry.

Traditional, vernacular architecture embodies Leopold's maxim to the tee. The vernacular is a human expression of a natural impression. The vernacular uses natural materials and traditional building skills and methods. The vernacular differentiates between regions, such as the contrasting house designs (noticeably dormer windows) of Badenoch and the Black Isle. Each region has a common template yet a particular signature. Modern houses tend to lack – sometimes to shockingly antiseptic levels – this sensitivity to place, this integrity. When a development is built in the vernacular, it lifts human spirits as something of beauty as well as grounding identity through stability. This is the challenge for architects and designers: to connect people to place through appropriate design.

Upstream from Tomatin I pitch the tent in a birch wood. Once the tent is up, preparation begins for an evening feast of Super Noodles and Orkney oatcakes – it's East meets West. For the first time in three days the midges come out in force. Midges: the bane of the Scottish Tourist Board, yet the original driving force behind the Highland fling. There are around 110 different species of midges in Scotland. Additional midge trivia includes the fact that a bat can eat up to 3,000 midges in an evening. From mid-May to mid-September, midges have the ability to turn a family holiday in Scotland into a Hitchcock-like nightmare.

Whilst Scottish folklore remains silent on the origin of midges, the Tlingit Indians of Alaska tell a story about the origin of mosquitoes. Mosquitoes, the Tlingit recount, are the ash particles of a human-eating giant who was killed by a warrior. After the giant was chopped into pieces and then burned over a fire, the warrior then threw the ashes into the air. At once the cloud of ashes became a cloud of mosquitoes, and from the midst of the cloud the giant's voice gave a laugh saying that he would eat people until the end of time.[170] Did midges originate from an ancient Scottish giant?

I haven't brought any midge repellent with me (stupidly), so it's a question of having to stay as covered up as possible and resorting to a technique of extending my lower jaw and puffing hot air around my face to blast away any biting creatures. To an onlooker this must look insane. I'd take midges over mosquitoes any day. I shall never forget the mosquitoes in Denali National Park, Alaska, that were so large you might think they were dragonflies. Mosquitoes that size could be enough to drive a non-smoker to tobacco – anything to keep away the agony. You can cover yourself in as much Deet as your skin can handle, but still they'll penetrate the chemical defence shield. Citronella and neem oil are more natural substances for repelling mosquitoes and midges. In the far north, however, real men wear Avon Skin-so-Soft. I always think of Monty Python's lumberjack sketch when I try to figure out how some logger in Pacific North West forests must have realised that a women's bath oil had insect repellent properties. Even more intriguing is how the said logger revealed the secret to his colleagues.

The next morning before starting out on the next section up to Coignafearn, I meet up with a friend who lives and works in Strathdearn. It's always good to see Donald. Unquestionably the coldest day of my life was spent in Donald's company back in January 1994. He had asked me upriver to help cull some hinds at the back of the season. That day had begun with a windless calm, the winter sun highlighting the diamond glints on the surface hoar of the snowpack. By early afternoon the wind had picked up from the west, bringing with it intermittent snow showers. Stalking deer invariably involves crawling through grass and peat in order to get a clear shot. In between the falls of snow we found ourselves wriggling on our bellies through the drifts. The final yards of each attempted stalk would then be thwarted by gusts of spindrift. It was a bitter day and showed me just how harsh the mountain environment of the Monadhliaths can be and how quickly conditions can change.

Donald is on his way up onto the hill to see if any grouse chicks have hatched. This time of the year is critical for grouse survival, and a persistently wet period or cold snap can diminish grouse stocks significantly. He tells me that tonight is going to be cold. I explain that I am off to the top of the Findhorn and am planning on camping up high in Coignafearn. Our cold day out stalking will prove good training, he tells me.

Heading further along the road that leads upstream, I think about how keen on stalking and shooting I used to be in my teens and early twenties. Today I choose not to stalk or shoot at all. My last day's stalking was near here in 1997. That day I pursued a stag across the hills of Strathdearn, having wounded it with my first shot. It took three bullets to finally kill the animal, and was an experience that made me feel sicker in the stomach and more wretched than anything I had ever done in my life. It was the first time I had ever wounded a deer, every previous occasion taking a single clean shot.

The experience triggered a change in my attitude towards the natural world. What that day taught me, looking back, was firstly my insincerity in hunting, and secondly just how out of balance the ecology of the Highlands has been for centuries. The majority of times when I stalked deer it was under the mandate of culling to help control numbers rather than taking 'for the pot' through engaging fully in the process of the hunt. With around 350,000 red deer in Scotland[171] – and some would argue that this figure is three times too many – deer numbers have to be controlled by humans to simulate the negative feedback loop that would typically have been provided by predators such as wolves. Culling to appropriate levels therefore protects habitats from over-browsing, helps prevent disease in the deer population, mimics natural selection when weaker and older deer are culled, and supports rare species such as golden eagles when grallochs are left on the hillside. Culling to control numbers, therefore, is a necessary practice for the contemporary condition, but should only be seen as a temporary measure until a better functioning system is in place.

It was the ecological imbalance of deer numbers (an imbalance created by humans) that formed my rationale for shooting deer – in other words, I took the position that my actions would be preventing further imbalance. Don't get me wrong, I'm not critiquing deer stalking per se nor the whole tradition and process of the hunt – far from it. Deer stalking provides an almost unparalleled opportunity to encounter intense wildness, be it the country you move through, the close proximity to wildlife, and not least the surge of adrenaline that races through your body when you move into position to take a shot. There is something, too, in killing the food that you will later eat that heightens your awareness of the place of human beings in the food chain and our reliance upon the natural world for our very sustenance. There is an honesty that involves taking ownership of your actions and witnessing the cycle of life and death. This is, I appreciate, a delicate area which some may view as dark and carnal. But humans who choose to eat meat are very much 'predators', and being part of the process in the provision of food – or at least knowing where your food comes from (beyond the supermarket shelf) – affords a certain humility and gratitude.

Culling simply to control numbers (rather than 'harvesting') strikes me as being a far from grounded, integral way of addressing things. Almost insubstantial, as if we are constantly trying to fight fire or stop the dam from bursting. Always trying to fix and maintain, instead of being in a position where we are encouraging the maximum diversity and stability of nature, and then harnessing and harvesting the abundance from that flow. Arguably, if we could reach a situation where deer numbers were lessened and non-human predators such as wolves were able to 'trim the range', stalkers might not have to devote so much time to culling deer numbers greatly in excess and could instead spend more time working to provide food and shelter for deer. The physical size of red deer could then begin to increase to the size they were centuries ago.[172] In the 17th century, red deer were reported to have been twice the size of the ones found today. As the forests that formed the natural range of red deer diminished, the deer were forced to areas above the tree line where they now largely remain. Up in these harsher zones, red deer cannot find the same provision of shelter and nutrients as is available in woods. We need to find a more permanent approach to deer management and conservation than currently exists in Scotland.

If we want to improve the quality of deer, we need trees.

If we want trees, we need to reintroduce mammals (wolves, beavers, bears and lynx).

If we have trees and large mammals we can prevent flooding, minimise climate change and encourage wild salmon.

Modern times have also seen a departure from the traditional practice and ritual of the hunt. The conservationists Sir Frank Fraser Darling and J. Morton Boyd summed up this situation when they warned that the potential exploitation of game stocks through sport in the Highlands would become more syndicated and commercialised and consequently lead to a loss of personal responsibility.[173] Elements of modern day field sports have become so overly commercial that the connection to hunting's original essence has been lost. One example is when pheasants are reared in vast numbers only to be shot for numbers' sake and where the emphasis is on quantity rather than quality.

When field sports drift more towards conspicuous consumption than grounded practice, the experience is shallower. The experience is more predictable than when there is a greater emphasis on wildness. Aldo Leopold developed a theorem that the recreational value of a head of game is inverse to the artificiality of its origin. In other words, the more intensive the system of game management which has produced the head of game, the less its value will be to a hunter. This theory holds as much validity today as it did in the 1930s when Leopold examined this issue.[174] The irony is that those who seek to alleviate the stresses of their working lives by a day out shooting enormous bags of game do themselves no favours by being in such a controlled setting. By manipulating the outcome, the genuine experience is lost.

An essential part of the process is what happens after an animal has been killed. Some people do not participate in

114

searching for a bird they have shot. Similarly, many that take part in deer stalking will not participate in the 'gralloch' when the deer is gutted. Instead, others are expected to find, pluck, gut, prepare, cook and eat the game that has been pursued. Those who participate in the whole process are likely to find the practice of hunting more fulfilling and sustaining. In Norway, the emphasis is far more upon hunting and fishing for food than for pleasure. Hunting in Norway – by contrast – would appear to be more rooted in cultural tradition than seems to be the case in the UK where corporate monoculture has been polluting an archaic experience.[175]

Lack of involvement in the whole hunting process and demands for large bags of game demonstrate disrespect to the animal in question, as if it is solely a commodity. This can only be counter-balanced by re-emphasising the cultural context of hunting. One of the best practices for strengthening this tradition is through ritual. In most regions in Europe where there is wild boar hunting, such as Bavaria and the Ardennes, the hunters engage in forms of ritual before and after a hunt. Ritual focuses the mind on what is about to take place, connects the hunter to a larger rhythmic identity, and is an act of reverence to the animal. My favourite description of a hunting for its alternative perspective on the hunting experience comes from the American poet Gary Snyder when he described how the Pueblo Indians would purify themselves in the days leading up to the hunt, taking 'emetics, a sweat bath, perhaps avoid their wife for a few days'. [176] The hunt would then be conducted with humility and would only take place if it was necessary to hunt an animal. The hunter would then improvise a song to the deer asking the animal be willing to die. Having shot the deer, the hunter would cut off the head of the deer and place it facing East, sprinkling corn around its mouth. Then the hunter would ask for forgiveness from the deer.

The shooting and stalking I experienced while growing up gave me an education into the countryside, were my first connection with mountain-craft, and provided the basis for my passion towards the natural environment. Henry Thoreau described this predicament more clearly than any other writer I have come across[177]

When some of my friends have asked me anxiously about their boys, whether they should let them hunt, I have answered, yes, remembering that it was one of the best parts of my education ... This was my answer with respect to these youths who were bent on this pursuit, trusting that they would soon outgrow it. No humane being, past the thoughtless age of boyhood, will wantonly murder any creature which holds its life by the same tenure that he does ... Such is oftenest the young man's introduction to the forest, and the most original part of himself. He goes thither at first as a hunter and fisher, until at last, if he has the seeds of a better life in him, he distinguishes his proper objects, as a poet or naturalist it may be, and leaves the gun and fish-pole behind.

Part of the Green movement found its roots in hunting (you only need to think of Aldo Leopold in the United States and a good number of conservationists in Africa, such as Ian Player), and this is something that is often overlooked. Rather than making a distinction between Greens and those involved with field sports, I would argue that it is essential that we should acknowledge the common ground. For the common ground is enormous. What tends to separate the two are issues such as fox hunting and protection of raptors which – and without meaning to belittle the emotive, ecological or legal significance of these two issues – are only the tip of the iceberg of contemporary environmental matters. Fox hunting can act as a smokescreen to finding this common ground. Before those who might together fight for the protection and well-being of the countryside engage with any opposition, in-fighting has left them exhausted, unfocussed and powerless. Meanwhile a political/economic agenda with little understanding of the subtleties, customs and rhythms of rural living sterilises the countryside.

Many Greens do not recognise the phenomenal knowledge and environmental wisdom that the likes of keepers, ghillies, stalkers and farmers possess. These people's knowledge of the environment is just as valuable as that of a scientific 'expert'. All too often, this grounded knowledge of the land is ignored in favour of academia. At a time when the natural environment – and from it the local economies and communities it supports – is under more pressure than ever, it's now that we need to build upon the similarities of those who care about the natural world and link grounded knowledge of the land with scientific research and effective political lobbying.

This focus on protecting the natural world and rural traditions also needs to extend to those involved in commercial activities that deplete and damage the natural world, but who then come to the countryside to seek sanctity in wild nature. When it comes to considering your ecological footprint on the planet, a key factor is the impact of your work on the environment. It makes no sense if our jobs destroy that which makes us feel most alive.

No matter what people's reasons or purposes for being in the countryside might be – to fish, ski, farm, garden, shoot, walk the dog, canoe, feed birds at a bird table, or even enjoy drinking a glass of clear, pure water or breathing a lung-full of fresh air – the fact is that so many of us share a love for the natural world in one way or another. That alone is reason to stand up and fight to protect and restore what gives life its substance and meaning.

This idea of a movement to promote the countryside's values, with all-inclusive respect for the many varied activities and lifestyles that exist within its context, can be found in Norwegian culture. Friluftsliv, literally meaning 'free air life', embodies a set of values that encourages meaningful connections between people and nature, and discourages commercial and/or technical imposition on the countryside.[178] In a sense, Friluftsliv encourages a pared-down approach to engaging with nature, maintaining that excessive equipment is merely a block to encountering the gifts and lessons that may be revealed. Friluftsliv has also played its part in influencing Norwegian politics through its ability to inspire people to think about themselves and nature in new ways.[179] This inclusive philosophy about how we can relate to and protect the land could work well in Scotland and go far towards enlarging identity and cultural awareness.

The road along the right bank of the river is flanked with birch, rowan and juniper. Sheep and cows graze the rough ground. Occasionally ewes with their lambs take flight at my presence on the road. But instead of turning off into the juniper and birch, the sheep will keep scampering on, sometimes for hundreds of yards. Each time I pause, hoping that my lack of haste will ease the sheep off the road. This is a game that demands patience and tolerance from both sides.

On both banks of the river sit a number of sporting lodges. Were these buildings named in admiration of the constructions of beavers, or was it the other way round?

STAGS OF STRATHDEARN

Reaching the bridge
At Dalmigavie
A snipe
Flits out
From the reeds

An oyster catcher
Sounds the alarm
Upstream
As a buzzard
Prowls the river bank

A deer fence encloses the trees at Glen Mazeran that stand between the road and the river. A sign reads: 'Findhorn River Riparian Woodlands'. The tree regeneration project is being jointly funded by the Forestry Commission and Glen Mazeran Estate, and managed by Scottish Woodlands.

As the valley tightens, the landscape darkens. Yet the river takes on a sparkle once again. Almost a cheekiness. Hill ponies feed on the far haugh. Stags in their hundreds mull on the plains. A pair of them box it out, rearing back on their hind legs and punching their hooves into each other's chest. Others trot with the poise of an Arab stallion – chest out, head tipped back.

As I leave Glen Mazeran, a JCB digs a ditch on the bank some two hundred yards below the road. I wave and within a few seconds the driver has switched off the engine, opened the cab door, and returned the wave.

'Is ma ditch straight?' he calls.

'Looks pretty good from up here,' I reply.

'Been here before?' he asks.

'A few times. I'm following the river,' I explain.

We watch an osprey recce the river for fish. The bird circles upwards on an air current, accelerating downwind on the north-westerly. The driver reaches into his cab and pulls out a set of binoculars. Ospreys are fairly easy to identify by the way in which they spiral without needing to stroke their wings. Also, the front of an osprey's wing is not straight and has a distinctive kink. After a few minutes, the osprey has finished surveying the territory and moves downriver.

I continue along the juniper-flanked road. The bracken here is three feet shorter than back at Glenferness.

> A heron
> Shadows the birches
> With languid wingbeat
> Pterodactyl-like

Upon reaching Coignascallan I bump into Alan and we chat for a while about my cup of tea with his mother, Margaret, yesterday. We also talk about a friend of mine whom Alan took stalking back in October. We then discuss the river. He asks me how far I plan to follow the river. I say that I'd like to find the source, and possibly travel up the tributary of the River Cro.

'Wild country,' he tells me.

There are five 'coigs' (or 'fifths') – small deposits of alluvial silts brought down by the burns – up here at the top of Strathdearn: Coignafearn ('The Fifth of the Alders'); Coignafeuinternich ('The Fifth of the Rank Grass'); Coignavullin ('The Fifth of the Mill'); Coignashie ('The Fifth of the Fairies'); and Coignascallan ('The Fifth of the Huts or Tents').

'The Fifth of the Huts or Tents' is a reference to the earliest hunter gatherers who lived in the area in tents made of deer hide[180] This practice appears so similar to descriptions of the Ihalmiut people, or 'People of the Deer', of the North West Territories in Canada that the theory of there once being a sub-Arctic culture seems all the more compelling[181] What is more, if an early Finn people came over from Scandinavia to Scotland, then were these the same people as those characters featured in the Ossianic legends?[182] In his book of essays, On Scottish Ground, Kenneth White describes the Finn tradition[183]

> The Finn tradition had been strong in Scotland, as in Ireland. For centuries, it had marked people's minds, and there were still traces of it in the landscape: the Fianna cliff (Sgor nam Fionnaidh) and Ossian's cave in Glencoe. On every crest of those mountains, says the legend, there's one of Finn's men sleeping – the wind is their breathing. Nowadays, we tend to see this tradition only in terms of its eighteenth-century romantic revival or its funny funeral by that garrulous literary undertaker, James Joyce. But if you trace it back far enough – up beyond Gaelic pieties – you come to something like an archaic deer-cult (Ossian, Finn's son, means 'fawn' and Oscar, his grandson, means 'deer-lover'), something close to the caribou cult of the Indians and Eskimo of Labrador. So much for distant origin, but by the time you come to the beginning of our era, the Fianna were a group of warrior-poets. To be a 'companion of Finn', you had to give up clan and family ties, be an accomplished athlete (run and leap faster than normal), and know by heart the twelve books of poetry.

The district of the five Coigs came to be known in ancient times as 'Schiphin', meaning 'Fairyland' or 'The Abode of Peace'.[184] 'Schiphin' doesn't sound too far away from the words 'ski' and 'finn', and the word skridfinn, the name attributed

121

by Paulus Diaconus who wrote around 750 AD of the people of Scandinavia that were 'hunters and skiers [and] who kept animals resembling deer (reindeer)'.[185]

White River clues.

Heading up the long straight from Coignascallan to the lodge at Coignafearn Estate, as stags cascade out from the birches and rocks and canter towards the river, you get this sense of wanting to continue further and further west. To Lochaber. To the Atlantic. There is something about being in high places – be it in Scotland, the Alps, the Himalayas, Patagonia – that creates a possibility of movement. That creates a space and a freedom.

At the far end of the straight, I see a vehicle heading my way. When it pulls up alongside me I recognise that it's Alec, one of the stalkers at Coignafearn, behind the wheel. We get talking about the weather and he tells me it will close in tomorrow. He also recounts that a salmon caught last week at Glen Mazeran still had sea lice on it – that's a good 50-mile swim from Findhorn Bay. I ask Alec about the source of the Findhorn. He tells me that if I choose to follow the River Cro, one of the two main headwaters of the River Findhorn, I will eventually come to an old fence that runs along the watershed.

Coignafearn was bought by its present owners in the late 1990s. While still promoting the traditional field sports of deer stalking and grouse shooting, Coignafearn is run strictly on ecological principles. Mile upon mile of high fences along the haughs have been removed to encourage birdlife. Areas of hill ground have been fenced using solar-powered electric fences to encourage native tree regeneration (with highly encouraging results), and wild flowers such as primrose and saxifrage are returning for the first time in decades. Bird boxes have been built throughout the estate. Most significantly, a programme of raptor protection and reintroduction has been encouraged. Coignafearn is well known for its golden eagles in particular, and virtually any dedicated bird watcher intent on seeing an eagle will have driven the road to 'Eagle Alley' at Coignafearn. Within this context of conservation, field sports thrive. Coignafearn is a genuinely pioneering model of how sporting estates can embrace nature conservation and ecology.

When I reach Coignafearn Lodge by the late afternoon, I meet some builders and painters I know from Forres and Nairn who are working on the refurbishment of the building. Although I knew that they might be working up here, none of them knew of my plans to walk up the river. They seem more than a little surprised to see me appear on foot. There can't be many houses in Scotland more remote than here. Jimmy, one of the joiners, thinks I'm slightly mad to be heading to a place even more remote than the lodge. 'Next chip shop's seventy miles away,' he warns me, 'in Fort William!'

> The river snakes
> Its way
> Through the grassy bowls
> Of mountains
>
> Aspen cling to banks
>
> A mountain hare
> With white feet
> Crouches
> Scratching its head
> With its right rear foot

At Dalbeg sits an old bothy, the most intact upriver building on the Findhorn. The last inhabitant was a man called Kerry Sinclair who lived here until the Second World War before moving to Spean Bridge. The bothy was used by shepherds from Strath Errick, as Charles St. John described from his visit here in the 1830s.[186]

I pitch the tent beside the boulders beyond Dalbeg. Boiling up a brew of tea after the long day's walk, I think about what might lie ahead tomorrow as I search for the source. Four days of walking thus far may not sound like a long journey, especially when you compare it to the pilgrimages people make to places like Mount Kailash in Tibet or when you think of the journeys that John Muir undertook when he crossed vast stretches of America. I can feel the distance, though, from the coastal fringe to the mountain interior and the frontier of watercourses that flow in different directions across the land. This journey reconfirms my conviction that without needing to travel all that far, we can find wilderness in Scotland.

I've never walked to the source of a river before, at least not as a goal. Most backcountry trips I've been on have been to ascend a mountain or traverse an expanse. Far more powerfully than a journey to mountain peak, I feel as if I am being drawn to the source of this river. Like following the life blood to the heart. I'm not sure what to expect tomorrow. I'm pretty sure there will be a lot of blanket bog to cross. Few trees. Hopefully no people. No visitor centre. No café. No casino. I'd like to find more space, even more space than I am witnessing now. Space that stretches to the horizon in all directions, where the wild has not been trimmed and tamed. Thirst-quenching, ecstatic space.

I glimpse a hind on the horizon peering down at me from the mountain top. Nobody passes unnoticed.

Remote, but not lonely. The river is home.

CHAPTER SEVEN

The Grey Mountains

'So remote the mountains,
Deer fearless enough
To come right up close
Tell me how far I am
From the outside world.'

Saigyo[187]

It has been a cold night in the mountains. Early June in these parts is a far cry from summer and I have woken a number of times to pull on more layers as well as a hat. There is a little bit of condensation in the tent, but at least it hasn't frozen. The time of the morning dew often seems to be the coldest part of the night. I reach across the tent for my thermos to pour a cup of tea, trying to perform the entire operation one-handed so that I don't leave the warmth of the sleeping bag.

I've only brought a summer sleeping bag to try and be as lightweight as possible, but a warmer bag would certainly have been welcome. My mind skips back to a trip I was on with a friend to Yosemite National Park in California in May 1994 when we camped along the snowline in Tuolomne Meadows. I had, stupidly, only brought a Mexican poncho to sleep under. My friend on the other hand chose to carry a 4-season down sleeping bag, the kind you would hope to have for a cold night in

Antarctica. My blurred memory of that night was my entire body shaking ceaselessly from nightfall to sunrise, and the occasional complaint from across the tent for me to stop shivering and chattering my teeth.

I eventually psych myself up enough to get out of bed, and open the door of tent to the sight of the river running its way through the mountains.

Morning brings
A sprinkling of rain
Could snow today

Gulls head upriver

Leaving the tent as it is, nestled below the windbreak of the boulders above Dalbeg, I continue along the track. A stubble of grey scree leaks from the upper slopes as if the mountains have been punctured by lightning bolts. Peat hags crown the mountaintops like cracks on dirty fingers. Curlew prepare for the day ahead, ranging the boggy ground in search of breakfast. A hare races over the grass as if late for an early morning meeting.

Am Monadh Liath – 'The Grey Mountain Range'. Thomas Henderson described these mountains as 'stark, chill and sombre', in contrast to the neighbouring Cairngorms. Although 'Gorm' means blue and is from the mountain of that name, the Cairngorms are Am Monadh Ruadh – the 'Red Mountains' – which at sunset 'sometimes glow with life, as if they held fire in their bosoms'.[188]

The Monadhliaths feel very different from the Cairngorms. Both ranges are as wild as you will find throughout Scotland, but the Monadhliaths seem more remote and less visited. The Cairngorms now form a national park, and correspondingly have increased their draw on visitors. Since the creation of the national park, real estate prices around the Cairngorms have risen significantly. The Monadhliaths lie largely outwith the national park, and despite increased recreation within the Cairngorm region do not have the same draw as the likes of the Lairig Ghru, Glen Feshie, Abernethy Forest, the Northern Corries, and areas on the other side of the Cairngorms such as Mar Lodge and Glen Derry, Glen Tilt and Drumochter.

Separating the honey pots of the Cairngorms and Loch Ness, the Monadhliaths are now being seen by the Highland Council and wind farm developers as a favourable location for wind power stations. Like a land that time forgot, or 'a land that could be industrialised without driving too many tourists away from the Highlands', the Monadhliaths face major change from renewable energy development in the coming years. When you consider Aldo Leopold's test of whether something 'will preserve the integrity, stability and beauty of the biotic community', these mountains are too fragile to absorb heavy industry. Wind farm developers often argue that because climate change is the biggest environmental issue we face, we must therefore allow wind farms to be erected in the windiest places of the Highlands, regardless of the fact that biodiversity may be adversely affected. We are told that we must sacrifice biodiversity and wild landscapes in order to prevent climate change. Such a proposition is a false choice. If in order to tackle the climate we destroy natural capital then we have failed. We have failed to move into the paradigm of genuine sustainable development, and have remained in a twilight existence of dysfunction and deception. Dealing with climate change and protecting wildlife and landscapes must all take place without any trade-offs.

A grouse gets up in a flurry and stutters its drill-like cry. As it rises out of the heather I catch sight of its scarlet eyelid. There can be few reds in the natural world as brilliant. The bird then banks clockwise on the wind and screams its way down river.

After a short while I come to the meeting place of the two main headwaters of the Findhorn: the Eskin and the Cro. The confluence is marked by a well-stained otter stone, as well as a number of large carved stones resembling giant chicken drumsticks and pelvic bones. The Eskin, meaning 'The Boggy Stream', is the shorter of the two tributaries and rises 'far to the West in as impenetrable a tangle of hills and gullies as there is in all Scotland'.[189] The Abhainn Cro Clach – 'The Water of the Stone of the Cattle' – starts many miles up into the backcountry south of Dalbeg.

The true source of the Findhorn is a question open to debate. Back in the 1930s Thomas Henderson in The Findhorn: River of Beauty sided with the River Eskin on the basis that it lay further to the west than the Cro.[190] Charles St. John, on the other hand, writing in 1837 in his Wild Sports and Natural History of the Highlands, was a River Cro man through and through, describing its glen as being 'beautiful in its grand and wild solitude', and a place seldom passed by 'the foot of man'.[191] In his 1911 The River Findhorn: From Source To Sea, George Bain sat on the fence and declared both places to be the actual source, explaining that: 'it is really formed by innumerable burns and water-flows descending from the mountain-side or issuing from a huge bog on an elevated plateau, and no particular spring can be identified as the fountain-head.'[192]

The stream less travelled. I opt for the Cro, the longer of the two waters. The Cro is about seven miles long from the confluence with the Eskin up to the edge of the watershed. At the least, I need to get up there and back to the tent by the end of today. I've decided to take a small pack with me and just carry the essentials – waterproofs, some warm clothes, food, thermos, first aid kit, map and compass – so that I can cover the ground more quickly.

Birch, aspen, willow and rowan hug the Cro's gullies, and their inaccessibility must frustrate the deer in the way that a display in a sweetie shop window might tantalise a child. These trees are relics of a time when most of the area of Strathdearn (excluding the mountain tops) was forested before being burned by accident – as the story goes – and then deliberately cleared to make room for 'poor crops and unskilful tillage'.[193]

Lichen the buff colour of hare fur capes the rocks. A kestrel takes off in a great hurry, zigzagging its way upstream. It looks at first like a merlin, but the feathers are too pink. Pink as the cliffs at Quilichan.

> Hinds patrol the high ground
> Where snow still fills the corries

Continuing along the track around the shoulder and hunched down under the summit of Scaraman, I see five swans ghost over the peat hags and snow pockets, steering the wind with their long necks. Minutes later three golden eagles paddle the air, circling like vultures, then vanish round the bend up into the high country as if knowing of some secret gathering upstream.

A little further on I come to the remains of an old bothy – what may have been part of a sheiling for the summer grazing

129

of cattle. A sheep's skull sits on the grass in the middle of the living-room floor. The old sheiling system in the Highlands would have been similar to the practice that continues today in Ladakh on the Tibetan Plateau where the livestock from every mountain village pass the summer on the high altitude grazing grounds. Some villages, such as the one I spent a summer in called Hemis Shukpachan ('The Place of the Cedars'), work a daily rota where each day a different family is responsible for driving the entire goat herd from the village up to the phu pastures. In addition, throughout the summer months, a handful of shepherds live up on the pastures in stone huts to watch over the yaks, dzos (yak/cattle cross), sheep and goats. The shepherds use slingshots – and their accuracy with these weapons is astonishing – to ward off Asiatic wolves and snow leopards in search of a free meal.[194] The livestock are then brought back down to villages for the autumn, winter and spring where they can dung the fields and, in the case of dzos, be used for ploughing. It is a system that has worked for at least a thousand years out there, and one which demonstrates the dynamic of cooperation in agricultural community life, creating employment and facilitating a way to raise livestock without having to destroy potential predators.

Whenever I come across a bothy in the Scottish landscape, I am invariably struck with just how beautifully it blends into its natural surroundings. It is not simply the use of stone and slate that creates this fluidity between built and natural environments, but the micro-locations of buildings – outwith the flood plains and below the exposed hill tops and ridges. It was once explained to me that when looking for a place to build a shelter (or pitch a tent), try and seek a spot that is a balance of yin (river valleys and feminine power) and yang (mountain peaks and masculine power).[195] Avoiding avalanche run-outs and the danger of any flash flood, this ancient concept of feng shui forms the most fundamental principle in planning. If ever you find yourself travelling through mountains in parts of the world where there are religious temples just take note of the purposeful location and sensitivity to place the buildings encapsulate. These places may well be 'power spots', too, harnessing the optimal energy of a place to create a sense of groundedness and strength. When people reinhabit abandoned bothies and help bring them back to life, there is magic in the reinvigoration. Like light returning to the shadows, and the song of the land being sung again.

Now the mountains are greener and more rounded than back at Dalbeg. Burns are divided into short waterfalls and step-like mossy stones. The Cro weaves a tight s-bend.

A stag antler
Lies in the peaty water
Upon a gravel bed

A gravestone
Stands at the end
Of the road
Where the deer track begins
No visible inscription
Too weathered

What a place
To be buried
Clear air
Eternal silence

The deer track traverses a planet of grass and mosses, sponges and anemones. The river straightens out under the supervision of Carn Ban. No wonder salmon try to return to tributaries such as the Cro to spawn – what a place to be born. Blessed from birth. Nevertheless, in recent years fewer and fewer salmon have been spawning up here, in part due to a lack of gravel as well as lack of tree life and therefore lack of the insects that are all so vital for juvenile salmonid survival.[196] My adventure upriver pales in comparison to the journey of a salmon and seems, frankly, so completely insignificant when you consider that this species swims downstream out into the sea and up to the Arctic feeding grounds off Greenland, before returning to the very same place of its birth to complete its life cycle. Next time you see a salmon leap, just think of the tall tales this voyager has to tell of great rapids and icy seas.

The stream is so small now that it can be criss-crossed to pick the best route. I find a lightning-stone, as I call them, charcoal grey with a white line through the middle. I keep a couple of these in my bedroom at home. Trophies of great spates. Antiques. But generally the stones are all jagged. In time the water will smooth and round them as they roll down to the coast. New mountains will in time form out at sea.

Dogen in his Sansuikyo, 'Scripture of Mountains and Waters', described this geological continuum of mountains eroding into the sea and forming in turn new mountains.[197] This principle of impermanency, one of Buddhism's central tenets, is exemplified constantly by the natural world. Letting go and accepting change are lessons we can learn from nature's flow. The Greek philosopher, Heraclitus, echoed this Eastern notion when he declared paradoxically that: 'Nothing is permanent but change'. Even mountains change over time, walking out to the ocean.

THE GREY MOUNTAINS

Glancing at the map last night to see if a source could be located, I noticed a lochan – Lochan na Cloiche Sgoilte, 'The Lochan of the Cloven Stone' – upon Carn Ban, but it sits somewhat below the height of land.[198]

> Movement is now by instinct
> Each tributary as wide
> As the mainstream
> Following whichever branch
> Seems the natural course

The creek tightens back into a canyon of spouts and pools, with rock walls clad in alpine lady's mantle and willow. Kelpie country.

It seems strange to think that 52 million years ago the River Findhorn was nearly twice its present length. Back then it is thought that the Findhorn was continuous with the River Moriston, draining the mountains on the Hebridean volcanic plateau.[199] Time takes on a whole new meaning in this context. In the land of fast food and urgent office deadlines, geological time is alien. Wrapped up in our own busy-ness, we rarely consider that the Earth is 4.5 billion years old, and that we are but transitory specks in the vastness of space. The brilliance of evolution can be unfathomable, as is just how we come to be where we are today. It is easier to tap into such thoughts miles away from concrete and clocks and newspaper headlines. Millions of years from now, this mountainside will no doubt look a different place. Perhaps covered by ice, by jungle, beneath the water. There is some comfort in knowing that even if we humans destroy our ability to live on the planet, the Earth will nevertheless continue evolving. That, however, is no excuse for failing to live in a more environmentally sound way. What we have around us is miraculous – we have everything we need – and it is for us to protect, restore and cherish this bounty.

Visibility is cut short in the dense cloud to 20 yards at best. I dare not leave the river's side lest I lose my way in a labyrinth of peat bogs. The slope begins to level off. What seem to be possible sources – large puddles, snow pockets, holes in the peat strata – are but false alarms. The urge to turn back fills me in countless bursts. How would people know if I didn't find the actual source? It's all the same up here – like some giant, indistinguishable piece of seaweed. But I would know, and I would wriggle in my bed at night for the knowledge that I stopped short. So I continue, like a man possessed, the rain now lashing across one side of my face.

> Finally I come to a place
> Where the stream of the water
> Is no wider
> Than the hoof print
> Of a stag
> A place
> Where the river
> Bleeds from the ground
> Where the skin of peat
> Turns to rock

The skeletal remains of an old iron fence run along the contour of the watershed marking the boundary of Coignafearn. A daddy-long-legs battles the wind to climb a tuft of grass. This is a land of cloud and stone, peat and snow, grass and wind. A place of silence.

THE GREY MOUNTAINS

I think of how the wind determines the destiny of a rain drop and which river course it will travel along. A gust from the north or east may mean a trip down the Spey, whereas the winds from the south and west could win you a journey down the Findhorn – two very different directions down to the same sea, where the clouds form and fly back to the mountains on the wind.

I think how fragile and innocent the river seems in its beginnings, but with the mountain, the wind and the rain for a family, the river could not wish for better nurturing and direction.

Does the river know at this point how wild and powerful it will become? Realise how so many will marvel at its beauty? Comprehend its importance to so many? On the rim of the watershed, the names of rivers that have captured my imagination since childhood spring forth:

> Mississippi, Amazon, Nile, Orinoco
> Tigris, Euphrates, Indus, Volga
> Yangtze, Limpopo, Cro, Po
> Cassley, Zambezi, Kali Gandaki
> Shin, Niger, Naver, Nairn
> Congo, Laxford, Lossie, Snake
> Oykel, Orange, Irawaddi
> Tatsenshini, Dorback, Elrick, Divie
> Mekong, Don, Deveron, Dee
> Piranha, Ohio, Tufaleofu
> Jordan, Narmada, Helmsdale, Ganges
> Eskin, Kawishiwi, Dulnain, Sunkosi
> Spey, Avon, Missouri, New
> Etive, Rhine, Back, Lune
> Volta, Rhone, Feshie, Zanskar
> Nimpkish, Nahanni, Findhorn

WHITE RIVER

Rivers all connected by the oceans and seas, the winds and the rains. The veins of the Earth. Their names alone conjure images of movement and beauty. The inhabitants of their banks, islands and deltas, the explorers, the ferrymen, listening to the music of the rivers' currents and then naming the sound, or basing the name upon the initial sight, or the mountain source, or the dream finally discovered.

Who was it that named the Findhorn? Was there a debate – did the river dwellers sit upon the sands under the pines tossing white mountain stones into the blackwater calling out ideas? Or sleep beside the whitewater awaiting the sound to form a name? Or was it the sea travellers arriving at the Culbin after crossing the North Sea, ecstatic at the distant sight of the white sands? Or was it because of the belly colour of oyster catchers, osprey, salmon and herons? Or because of gulls, or the tail of the roe? Or because of the moon? Or because of the white of the clouds in the morning light?

For the first time in my life I feel as if I am beginning to understand the River Findhorn. From now on, whenever I gaze upon the river downstream, whether flowing with the ink black roar of a snow melt, with the bluebottle sheen of a spring morning, with the peaty red brindle in the warm light of summer, or with the muddy thunder of an autumn spate, I will know where it's coming from.

I dream of a day when the watershed of the River Findhorn has been reforested, when the howl of wolves can be heard on moonlit winter nights, and when wild salmon return to the river in abundance. Because that day will be a great day. It will be a day when we human beings have come to see our true place in the interconnectedness of the world, and have been moved to act upon that consciousness. It will be a day when we start to inhabit the Earth with a grace. Like a river.

After a short while the cloud lifts and the sun comes out. At last the threads of water burrowing into the Cro can be seen. In the sunlight, the vastness of the high ground is revealed.

Cobwebs of dew
Stretch
Between the grass-tips

A snipe
Kites
On the wind
Then tucks down
To the hags

Setting off downstream with a new lease of energy in the clear light, I pick a speedier route across the back of Scaraman, before joining the track down to Dalbeg. If I can reach Coignafearn Lodge before late afternoon, I may just manage to hitch a ride with the construction crew back down river. As soon as the conditions for paddling are right, I'll then begin the downstream part of the journey by canoe from Tomatin.

CHAPTER EIGHT

Down through the Streens

'There is magic in the feel of a paddle and the movement
of a canoe, a magic compounded of distance, adventure,
solitude and peace. The way of a canoe is the way of
wilderness and a freedom almost forgotten.'

Sigurd Olson, The Singing Wilderness[200]

It is now some three weeks since I was in the Monadhliaths at the
head of the river. I've left my car downstream below Drynachan
and have hitched a lift along with my canoe to Tomatin. Loading
up the canoe with safety gear for today's paddle, I inspect the
water as it runs through the strath.

White diamonds
In the blackwater
Night sky
Riding the land
From mountain to sea

In those first few strokes away from the shore, land-based
fears of a river environment disappear. By the time the canoe
reaches the main current of the River Findhorn and minor
adjustments of weight, balance and body position are complete,
the rhythm of the paddle finds its groove, and everything melts
into the river's dark belly.

DOWN THROUGH THE STREENS

The apprehension before a canoe journey on the River Findhorn is never something I've been able to ignore. It's part of the process. Some nights it can grip like a fever.

The power of spates
Hurtling
Down from the mountains
On days
When rain
Seemed a thousand miles
And a season away

Moments
Pinned broadside
To a rock
Canoe tipped
On its downstream edge
Whitewater
Frothing
From the black

Where human voices
Yell
Unheard
Only the stereo bellows
Of the river
Dropping down
Ecstatic
Over contours
To pools of black silence

The fever focuses the mind. What equipment is needed? Where are the safety exits en route? What could happen in a split second, demanding immediate resolution? What if the canoe sinks miles away from help? Plans made a week or day before are called before the jury on the morning of a trip. Have you thought about the height of the water? It's up half a foot – the rapids will have changed their composition, maybe even called in a few more waves. It's dropped a foot overnight – it'll be bumpy in the rock gardens, may have to get out and push in places. Have you seen the forecast? There's rain moving in from the west, should hit the Monadhliaths by mid-morning. Could mean a wall of chocolate water, trees at the vanguard.

The blackwater, White River fever.

The simple answer to the fever is to stay indoors. Or go paddle on a loch. Or find another river. If it's been raining anything more than a shower – or if there has been rain in the mountains – I won't go out on the Findhorn. When I was younger I remember two occasions out fishing when the spate rushed in like the wind, besieging the island I was standing on. The speed and uncontrollability of what happened was terrifying, and taught me never to disrespect the unfathomable power of the river.

So what about the days when the river runs at a good height for paddling? If it hasn't rained in the past 24 hours, then what's stopping you?

Crossing the threshold. The knowledge that once over the threshold the experience will (quite possibly) change your perception of the river, alter your reality in the world, and bring you closer to understanding who you are. It's the risk involved in entering new territory. That you are about to change. As Tom Robbins wrote in Fierce Invalids Home from Hot Climates:

140

DOWN THROUGH THE STREENS

There are times when we can feel destiny close around us like a fist around a doorknob. Sure, we can resist. But a knob that won't turn, a door that never budges, is a nuisance to the gods. The gods may kick in the jamb. Worse, they may walk away in disgust, leaving us to hang dumbly from our tight hinges, deprived of any other chance in life to swing open into unnecessary risk and thus into enchantment.[201]

Why is it that the River Spey does not conjure up the same 5am tribunal for me as the Findhorn, especially seeing as the Spey is a bigger river and its current faster flowing than its sister? The mythologist Joseph Campbell once explained that whenever someone enters a place which to them is sacred – be it a church, mountain, temple, river – the individual must pass the threshold guardians, gatekeepers whose role is to drive away those incapable of reaching the higher realms within.[202] At the moment of entry the individual undergoes a metamorphosis. Every temple has its gargoyles, but if the place is not sacred to you it is unlikely that you will notice their presence and therefore not undergo the transformation.

I consider the River Findhorn a sacred place.

So how do you bring yourself to the threshold? How do you make that step across the abyss into the other world? For me, it's a case of trying to replace the fear with some kind of faith. Asking the river for safe passage. Asking for deliverance.

Heading out from the bridge at Tomatin, the river runs a straight line through the haugh fields. Fishing groynes create a slalom course as they jetty into the current, each one's wing-stone lurking just below the surface. The wind is strong today. Blowing upstream from the north-east. It's going to be a hard day with the paddle.

141

WHITE RIVER

The canoe I'm paddling is a Mad River 'Teton'. It's a solid boat, necessary for the likes of the Findhorn where you are likely to bump into rocks. It's very stable too and can carry a great deal of equipment. It is a heavy boat, however, compared to most others on the market, which makes 'portaging' (when you carry the canoe on your shoulders) a real challenge. When I first bought my canoe I hadn't done that much river paddling at all. I had previously spent a month paddling through the Boundary Waters of Minnesota and Ontario with Voyageur Outward Bound School when I was 19, and it was there that I fell in love with the complete freedom that canoeing provides. Up in those ancient Ojibway lands and waters beyond the Kawishiwi River, I learned how close you can come to wildlife (moose, bear, bald eagles, beaver) when you travel by canoe, and that you can bring far more food for an extended backcountry trip than you might otherwise be able to do on foot or by ski in the mountains. I experienced, too, how blissfully far away from civilisation the canoe can carry you.

The former Canadian Prime Minister, Pierre Elliott Trudeau, who spent time paddling the Nahanni River in the North West Territories with the grand master of modern canoeing, Bill Mason, summed up the tonic of canoe travel so poignantly when he stated:

> What sets a canoeing expedition apart is that it purifies you more rapidly and inescapably than any other. Travel a thousand miles by train and you are a brute; pedal five hundred on a bicycle and you remain basically a bourgeois; but paddle a hundred in a canoe and you are already a child of nature.[203]

I move all the gear towards the bow to alter the trim and minimise the weathervane effect. You'd think that travelling with the river's current would create enough momentum to override the efforts of the wind, but the wind can be one of the most critical factors when canoeing on a river. As you line up for the deep-water 'V' at the entry to a rapid, a gust of wind can flick the boat off course into a rock and swing you broadside.

Today I'm paddling from Tomatin down to Banchor un–accompanied. It's certainly not what canoeing associations endorse, and many would view paddling in this manner as plain foolishness. I fully heed the warnings, and most of my time out paddling I go with a companion. Having weighed up the risks involved for this section, I've decided that going alone will allow a greater opportunity to learn about the river more intimately. The canoeist-explorer Robert Perkins once described how travelling alone, particularly into a wilderness, can be risky, but that just as risky is not to follow your dreams.[204] There is something unparalleled about paddling alone. The legendary Canadian outdoorsman Calvin Rutstrum summed it up for me when he wrote that our most profound moments generally occur when we are alone, and that we do not become intruders to the natural world but more part of the natural order.[205]

Going solo lessens the footprint but means heightened concentration and greater attention to the immediacy of what surrounds you. Going solo requires silence and no talking – the key to entering a level of discourse with the natural world. Where you hear the music of the rapids, of the oyster catcher, of the wind in the aspen, of the splash of the salmon's belly. Where you become aware of the life around you. Of the song of which you are part, and which you can learn to sing.

Dropping into the deep bend at Inverbrough, a dog on the far bank starts barking at the canoe. The golden Labrador seems a little bemused, howling out that some strange looking 16-foot-long green boat has just arrived in its territory. The dog's owner walks down the grassy bank. The dog looks at the owner, barks a few times looking back at me on the water, and then calls off the alarm. I pull into the eddy for a chat. The owner asks how far I'm heading. I tell him that I'll go through the Streens today, but that my plan is to make it back to the coast in due course. He tells me that he's never been in a kayak. I tell him that this is a canoe. I try to explain the obvious differences between canoes and kayaks: kayak paddles tend to have double blades, kayaks generally have enclosed cockpits, and kayaks originate in Greenland and the Arctic whereas the open canoe is a progression of the type paddled by Native Indians. We discuss the height of the water and how it has dropped almost a foot since this time yesterday. He explains that he and his wife have come here to fish the following week. Today is Sunday, which means no fishing. A river free of fishing lines where the canoeist can drift with one less obstacle to worry about.

There's been considerable tension during the past 30 years about access to rivers in Scotland for canoeists. Many fishermen maintain that canoeists are responsible for the decline in wild salmon stocks. Some fishers on the River Spey have argued that disturbance to a 'holding pool' may affect the behaviour and development of salmon at the smolt stage – the period when the fish are thought to develop their ability to recognise the stream of their birth to which they eventually try to return.[206] To this extent, paddling in low water does possibly exacerbate the situation. It would be interesting, however, to see a proper environmental impact assessment of these assertions as the science surrounding the debate does not yet seem to be in existence.

My own overall sense is that canoeists and kayakers have

been made the scapegoats of a much larger, more complex problem that needs to be addressed. They are easy targets upon which to pin blame born from frustration. Personally I've never had any truly heated encounters with people fishing on rivers such as the Findhorn and Spey (well, there was that one time on the Spey when some friends in a canoe behind me managed to broadside a fisherman and land him in their boat, rod and all ...), and maybe it's because I prefer to paddle either solo or in a small group. But generally I've found anglers on the Findhorn and Spey to be fairly accommodating to canoeists.

A large part of the problem is lack of education into the other pastime. I maintain wholeheartedly that canoeing will improve a fisherman's knowledge of a river and how water moves, and equally I believe that any true canoe or sea-kayaking trip involves you catching your own fish. People often approach their time on the river with an attitude that it is their 'right' to be there, and that no one is going to get in their way – hence the insecurity, the defensiveness, the aggression. It is worth noting, though, that there has been significant progress locally to improve fishing– paddling relations.

It comes down to the basics of communication and respect for another's space. Paddlers need to try to make signals to a fisherman in good time to negotiate the best route for the canoe and to avoid disturbing the water being fished – either tucking in behind the fisherman, or travelling out wide to the far side of the river. Fishermen need to realise that there may be beginners amidst the paddling group who are maybe nervous and trying their hardest to control their boat away from your space. A smile, even a 'hello' (kindergarten stuff really), can go a long way to remove any unnecessary tension.

We read in the newspapers every day about wars in the Middle

East, fighting in Africa, trade embargoes and so on, and peace is often portrayed as some quicksilver, macro impossibility. Peace starts at the very most basic level, firstly within ourselves and then through one-to-one interaction. Without calm foundations, peace hasn't got a chance. It's how we treat other people. Are we prepared to have the self-confidence and equanimity to greet the stranger, to tolerate their differences, or are we to continue the cycle of hostility? The river is a model where we can practise tolerance. Nobody 'owns' the river, whatever human laws might suggest. We are all guests of the river. All of us who spend time in the river's presence are part of a wider community, ranging from the mountains to the sea.

One of my favourite types of canoe trip is when I'm joined by someone whose primary contact with rivers is through fishing, and who has never journeyed in a canoe before. It requires a level-mindedness from the fisher and an acceptance that they might receive flack from those who cannot fathom why anyone in their right mind would ever want to ride in a canoe. But no matter how much hassle they might receive from family and friends before coming along, it is guaranteed that their smile at the end of the trip will ward off all slings and arrows. All you need to do is introduce them to the river, and let it work its spell.

There is obviously the thrill of travelling down white water. Then there's the calligraphy of paddle strokes with those mesmeric tiny whirlpools that form in their wake and then vanish back into the surface. Most significant is the new perspective of the river that canoeing brings to a fisherman. You see the river in a completely different light. Feel its speed. Watch the surface movement with an intense study, reading the rock-ledge shallows, the shingle, the deep-water channels, eddies, stoppers and pillows. Like the Sami of Northern Scandinavia who continue to use specific terms and words to describe the composition and patterns of the water, a fisherman who travels by canoe relearns the ancient art of river-reading.

The 19th-century American painter Winslow Homer captured the essence of the relationship that is possible between fly rod and canoe in his paintings of the Adirondacks and Quebec. He demonstrated that fly fishing and canoeing were always meant to live together in balance and with deftness. Inspired by Homer's images, I've taken a good friend trout fishing on a loch in the canoe a number of times before, partly to prove the point that canoeing need not scare away fish, but also to show that the canoe is the ultimate vessel from which to fish. The magic of the fly rod, the meditation of paddling the silent Indian stroke with a beautiful wooden paddle. Being closer to the water in the canoe than in a rowing boat, the fisher truly feels part of the ecosystem, almost poised over the water like a heron. You are able to unleash a cast far more freely from a canoe than from a bank where you might be inhibited by trees. The manoeuvrability of the canoe means that playing a trout becomes a capoeira-like dance of attack, defence and counter-attack. And the canoe stalks the water in silence, without the creaking clatter of oar rollicks.

So when we think of a river such as the Findhorn, which has so many pools that are inaccessible to fishermen given the limitations of wading or fishing from a rowing boat, it seems perfectly logical to me that the true way to fish the Findhorn is from a canoe. You could fish an entire beat in a day; if you hooked a salmon which then took off downstream into another pool you could follow it by canoe; and let's not forget that you wouldd also experience the thrill of running the whitewater. Both canoeing and fly fishing, when pared down to the essential, offer a rare chance to experience the natural world at a profound and captivating level. It seems so strange that this polarity between canoeing and fly fishing exists in the United Kingdom, when in places such as Canada canoes are the fly fishing vessel par excellence. If you love fishing but have never fished from a canoe, then I'm sorry you've been missing out.

> Approaching Ruthven
> Ten thousand gulls cry out
>
> Parr jump, bank-side
> Shingle turns to rock
>
> Arctic terns stream the air
>
> Large-girthed birch trees
> Crowds of juniper
>
> Ahead lie the Streens
> And the high crags
> Of wolf country

A heron leapfrogs its way down the pools. It pauses, watching me try to negotiate the underwater rocks hiding in the dark like bandits, then moves on ahead round the next bend.

A merganser mother decoys me away from her chicks, leading me into the deep-water entry to Shenachie.

In Gaelic the word seanachaidh means 'the reciter of tales or stories'. This place certainly has its stories, that's for sure. But what about the music for the tales? Whatever happened to the songs and how did they sound?

I've never heard any tunes from the River Findhorn. I've heard many from the west and from the Isles, from Strathspey and from Aberdeenshire. But none from this river. The songs may have left the area during the Highland Clearances when there was an exodus from Strathdearn to Georgia. Maybe the music found sanctuary in the mountains of Appalachia, and along the coast lines of Cape Breton. How incredible it would be to find these songs once again and to bring them home, as has been done in other parts of the north.

> To play them outdoors
> Plant trees
> And let all the springs run again

When we talk of a music of place we touch upon human ecology in its purest form. Mental composition mirroring the lines of the landscape, conveying the emotion of human reactions to a place. Blending natural fibres with human craft and energy to create a sound.

Starting with instrumentation, there's a saying that Scotland can (roughly) be divided into two areas in terms of musical geography. There's piping in the Gaelic-speaking areas of the west and north west, and the fiddle playing of the north east and further south (there is Shetland too, of course). The River Findhorn has its share of both.

> Horsehair on wood
> Goat stomach
> Reeds and wind

In terms of composition and musical notation mirroring the physical landscape of the river, there isn't the steadiness of a Strathspey in the Findhorn. The Findhorn certainly isn't a march – if anything it's unregimented. A jig in parts, for sure. A reflective air in some places, maybe, but there's little room on the water to pause and reflect, save the moments when it gathers itself before some of the big rapids – the river is almost always moving on and on, but rarely stopping for breath.

If we study the movement of the water, the fast-flowing surges and squeezes of the Findhorn, the type of music it conjures most strongly for me is bluegrass. I'm thinking dragonfly-wing banjo breakdowns à la Earl Scruggs, Béla Fleck, John Hartford, Eric Weissberg. The whitewater-tumbling dobro slides of Jerry Douglas. The intricate mandolin-picking lines of Bill Monroe, Dave Grisman, Sam Bush and Chris Thile.

The first music I ever heard that instantly made me think of the River Findhorn was back in 1995 when I was studying at the University of North Carolina at Chapel Hill. One of my flat-mates played guitar in a bluegrass band, and one evening lent me an album that would catapult me into a whole new galaxy of music. It was The Telluride Sessions by Strength In Numbers. The band's all-star line-up of Sam Bush on mandolin, Mark O'Connor on fiddle, Béla Fleck on banjo, Edgar Meyer on bass, and Jerry Douglas on dobro created a sound so novel to me, yet a sound that I felt I had been waiting to hear my entire life. The style of the album, and also much of the musicians' other works, fits more into the genre of 'newgrass'. Acoustic jamming at the ultimate calibre.

So maybe we could start with a bluegrass/newgrass style model for pipes and fiddles. What's stopping us from adding the other instruments typically featured in Celtic music such as the accordion, whistles, bhodran, clarsach, piano and guitar? Mix them into the cauldron too.

DOWN THROUGH THE STREENS

How about adding instruments from further afield to create to a River Findhorn sound? I mean, if we look at the non-human constituents of the larger community we get geese and salmon that spend time in the Arctic. Surely that connects us to the wooden flutes and cowhorns of Scandinavia, as featured in the music of Swedish multi-instrumentalist Ale Möller (for example Fully Rigged featuring Möller with genius Shetland fiddler Aly Bain). When we consider the ospreys that winter in West Africa, that connects us to the percussive depth of the djembe drum (amongst others). How about some kora thrown into the mix too, Toumani Diabate style?

West Africa is also the homeland of original banjo music with the ribek. The ribek travelled to America and to the Caribbean. The osprey completes the triangle then, bringing banjo music to the River Findhorn. Something I find fascinating about bluegrass banjo is that it is the dialectic of a white cultural interpretation and application of an originally black instrument, so to speak: the flip-side of be-bop and hard bop saxophone playing such as the music of Charlie Parker and John Coltrane – African Americans interpreting and applying their cultural root rhythms to a Belgian invention. But it's in that cross-over – that trade of instruments to places distant from their roots where their sound resonates with a new interpretation and application – where the energy lies.

> That rapid exchange
> Of black into white
> And white into black

The canoe drops through the whitewater at Shenachie as I pass the steep mountain of Cnocan Mór. Then across the fairy pool of

Pollochaig, and on through the narrows into Cawdor. I shore up
on a small beach just upstream from Kincraig, which will form
an ideal spot for lunch. The wind has changed direction from
earlier and now blows downstream. The afternoon's paddling
should be less of a battle with the elements.

I've got the idea of river music echoing through my mind.
Conveying the sound of water through writing is such a
challenge because river music out-dances prose. Only the most
free-ranging poetry can begin to capture the river's essence.
To write like flowing water. That is the space, the expression.
When your very awareness of life's parameters reaches a new
dimension. Where mud lies under your skin. Where you shake
the ice water from your hair. Where pine resin pumps through
your veins.

> Paddling on
> Past Kincraig
> And Ballachrochin
> Ballagan and Quilichan
> The world feels
> A wide open place –
> Archipelagos of cloud
> Sub-Arctic space

On the rapid before the bridge to Tirfogrean, where the river
narrows around a large rock, the canoe pinballs its way off the
rocks in the left channel, almost flipping as the boat lands in the
deep, dark pool. Rapids can be deceptive.

The section past Drynachan Lodge and Carnoch is a giant rock
garden. On several occasions the canoe bellies out on boulders,
and each time I have to climb out and wade, towing the canoe

into a deeper channel where I can begin paddling again. This is one aspect of canoeing unaccompanied that does unnerve me – the fact that I could get my foot stuck under a rock.

There's another pinballing rapid at the steep Scots pine bank of Creag an Fhithich. Here the river lunges over the rocks, the white stones on each bank squeezing the water on ever faster. In hindsight I should have lined the boat through this gap or portaged.

I end the first section downstream opposite Dalbuie. It's going to take me three more stretches to paddle the navigable part of the river. The section I've just been through is rarely paddled, and even rarer is to find someone paddling the section from Coignafearn to Tomatin. You would have to paddle that part on a dropping spate, and that's not something I'm willing to do given the Findhorn's unpredictability. The next three sections are more frequently paddled, these being known as the Upper (Banchor to Dulsie), Upper Middle (Dulsie to Ardclach) and Middle (Ardclach to Randolph's Leap), and I'll combine these into two by paddling from Banchor down to Ardclach. You then have the most technically challenging part of the river known as the Lower (Randloph's Leap to Sluie), which I'll have to skip as my trusty green canoe would never squeeze through the tight turns and chutes. Following this logic, the section I have just been through from Tomatin to Banchor might be called the Upper Upper, and final section from Sluie to the sea the Lower Lower.

Rightly or wrongly, I've decided not to carry my camping gear on the trip back downstream, which means I can travel as lightly as possible in the boat and have increased manoeuvrability in the whitewater sections. Instead I'll return home tonight and return to the river to paddle the next section soon. The ideal would have been to paddle the entire river from Coignafearn to the sea, tackling the section between Randolph's Leap and Sluie, and to do it in a continual journey stocked up with food for a few days and camping gear. Choosing the craft to paddle a river such as this on a continual journey is a tough balancing act – on the one hand you need something nimble, on the other you need capacity to carry gear.

The river has been dropping throughout the day on the tail of a spate which passed through 48 hours ago. It's been a good height for paddling solo, but you'd never manage two people in a canoe at this height. Technically there has been nothing particularly demanding. Paddling solo and unaccompanied, though, means you have to concentrate intensely. I am exhausted, but it feels good nevertheless to have travelled back through the big sky country of Strathdearn and the Streens.

CHAPTER NINE

Into the Dragon's Teeth

'Mishe-Nahma, King of Fishes
In his wrath he darted upward
Flashing leaped into the sunshine
Opened his great jaws and swallowed
Both canoe and Hiawatha.'

Henry W. Longfellow,
The Song of Hiawatha VIII[207]

Back at Banchor once again a few days later, I prepare the canoe for the second section downstream that will take me under Dulsie Bridge and down through Glenferness to Ardclach. On the journey upstream I chose to follow the road from Dulsie to Drynachan, and so this part of the river is new territory to me.

Just after setting off on the water, a dipper darts across the current in front of the canoe. It lands on a rock, bobbing back and forth as it scans the water. As the canoe draws level, the bird then zips towards an eddy, plunging its chestnut body into the water. I turn my head to watch where the dipper might surface, but with the canoe moving into faster water must instead fix my attention downstream.

Before the bridge at Banchor the rocks funnel the river through a narrower gap. Rowans hug the gneiss slabs. Here the canoe bounces through a series of short pools. The Banchor Triple.

WHITE RIVER

The last spate has left its signature of flattened mellick grass pointing upstream in places where giant eddies have formed in the high water. Turf has also been peeled back like a rolled-up carpet under the water's workings, as the riverbank has been eroded to dirt slopes.

Sturdy aspen inhabit the region before the mouth of the Tor Burn. Soon after the burn lies a long, winging, right-hand chute of a rapid that lunges the canoe forward at high speed. A sharp rock lurks just beneath the surface on the left of the tail. Fail to pick the right line, and you may find yourself mending canoe punctures on the shingle.

I choose to line the next rapid via its right channel where the river splits around a stony island. The hillock at Dulsie stands above the trees on river right. A rock face resembling a Polynesian tiki appears as the river moves through a haunting set of deep, dark pools.

The grilse are jumping today.

The river then gathers speed towards the rapids at Dulsie. I pull ashore on the stony island before the first of the two big rapids. My initial thought is to line the first rapid on river left at the hairpin, then paddle across to river right to portage the second rapid, which drops into the pool at Dulsie Bridge. But I quickly have to change my plan. At the first rapid there is no way I will be able to line and wade across from the island to the far bank. It would be too dangerous. The river is fairly high today and it's here, peering into the roar of the first rapid – almost like staring into a volcano – that I decide to retrace my steps and track the canoe back upstream a hundred yards. After a ferry glide to the right bank, I exit and portage down to the bridge.

The rapid at Dulsie with all its power and spill and noise empties its energy into the silence of the pools just below the bridge. I marvel at the juxtaposition of fury and calm in a river. There is hope in knowing that for every rapid in life there is a stretch of serenity somewhere around the bend. Then again, just when you think life is nothing but smooth and all under control, it lets fly into turbulence.

The rocks below Dulsie sit in anarchic configurations, crafted by the water's ceaseless carving and hammering. The water seems like a black hole stretching down into the depths of the Earth. Here and there the water slips in a 'V' above gravel beds. Alders stud both banks. A series of narrow channels and rocky shelves lead to the Silver Fir wood beside the Princess Stone. On the left stands the last field for the next couple of miles as the river runs through the heart of Glenferness. The banks tighten into the Scots pine clad palisades around Leven's Gorge.

I choose to portage the gorge with its tight switchback. Some bends just weren't carved for 16-foot-long Canadian canoes. It is a fantastically impressive rapid, squeezing its way through gaps and hurtling over drops, opening up into a timeless amphitheatre of water, rock, pine and sky.

The portage is the longest I have made so far on the river, about 70 metres downstream to a point where I reload the gear. Portaging is all part of the canoe experience. As Bill Mason once pointed out, each portage sets you further away from civilisation and deepens the wilderness experience.[208] Many abhor the idea of having to carry equipment across country to the next section of water, but I adore it. Carrying a canoe on your shoulders signifies that you are out there, journeying under your own steam and within your own timeframe.

There are a couple of different ways to lift a canoe onto your shoulders: if you happen to have a friend at hand, they can lift the bow of the upside-down canoe and create an 'A-frame' while you scurry underneath the boat and fit your shoulders and neck around the yoke thwart. When no one is around to help, though, the most straightforward way is to position the boat upright, stand at one side of the centre of the canoe, reach across and grab the far gunwhale with the arm closest to the bow, roll the canoe first onto your thighs and then, with a jerk akin to a weightlifter's, flip the canoe over your head and onto your shoulders. Anyone watching will marvel at your seeming brute force, but in truth it's all about technique. Then off you go, following the portage trail to the next navigable stretch of water.

The voyageurs in Canada who worked for the Hudson Bay Company and North West Company in the 18th and 19th centuries paddled enormous 36-foot-long canoes laden with supplies and furs. The larger canoes – the 'canots de maitre' – would set off from Montreal when the ice melted each spring, and head to Grand Portage on the western shores of Lake Superior. Grand Portage was the main gateway into the interior and a key trading post. French-Canadians made up the majority of the voyageurs, and those that travelled this section out from Montreal were known as 'mangeurs du lard' (literally 'eaters of fat') because they were considered not quite so hard core as their counterpart 'hivernants' ('winterers') who paddled shorter 25-foot canoes ('canots du nord') from Grand Portage further west into the Canadian interior.

The voyageurs paddled for 14 hours a day, and would put in a couple of hours before breakfast. Galette or bannock (a type of flat bread), pemmican (dried meat with fat and dried fruit mixed in) and pea soup were the staple diet. To combat the mosquitoes, the men would coat themselves in skunk oil and bear grease, and smoke their pipes at every break they took. You can only imagine the smell. The brigades would sing songs on the water to take the mind off the strain of paddling, and there were songs too for the portage trails.

The voyageurs' canoes were larger models of the traditional canoes paddled by the Native Indian tribes in the east of Canada. The Abenaki, Ojibway, Cree and Algonquin were celebrated designers of canoes, each tribe with its own particular differentiation. Birch bark was the material used for the skin of the canoe, and white cedar was the wood selected for the frame. This style of canoe was very different from those built by tribes in the Pacific North West, such as the Haida, Tlingit and Kwakiatul, who created dug-out canoes from Western red cedar and were renowned for their enormous war canoes.

The man who became the first person to cross the continent of North America north of Mexico by canoe was neither Native Indian nor French-Canadian, but a Scot from the Outer Hebrides. Alexander Mackenzie, born in Stornoway on the Isle of Lewis, became Canada's most emblematic explorer when in June 1793 he arrived on the Pacific coast near Bella Coola in modern day British Columbia. Mackenzie opened up a commercially viable route to the Pacific Ocean, and paved the way for the expansion of Canada's economy.[209]

This section of the river reminds me strongly of the Yukon. Maybe it's the dense atmosphere of the surrounding forest, or the colour of the trees, or the lines of the rocks. Or perhaps it's just that the Yukon conveys an idea of wild space. I was lucky to travel there in 1997 when a friend and I drove my beaten-up 1974 Plymouth Volaré, called Nellie, from North Carolina to Alaska and back – 16,000 miles in seven weeks. The Yukon – of all the places on that trip – cast a spell on me, a place of vast forest above which mountain ranges stood visible in their entirety from end to end, and a place of formidable rivers.

Paddling this part of the river you travel in anything but a straight line. Not only does the course of the river – when you look at it on the map – bend and double-back, but the fall-line also weaves at 90 degree turns within this space. Snappy 'pry' and 'draw' paddle manoeuvres are often required to line up the canoe with the 'V' channels as you stack in the upstream holding pool, preparing to slip down into the next short rapid. There is a delicious sense of exhilaration in these short runs, as the canoe ghosts along the flow.

I have been fascinated – ever since I took up whitewater canoeing – with the idea of 'flow'. There is the route that water takes as it flows downstream in its path of least resistance, which the Taoists consider the role model and metaphor for how we humans might aspire to live.[210]

There is the process of flow that psychologists such as Carl Rogers have remarked is the 'richest and most rewarding' experience that humans can move within, and where life 'is always in process of becoming'.[211]

The definition of flow that articulates the essence of travelling through whitewater – that sense of total bliss when you are riding the rapids in a torrent of unchecked exhilaration and abandonment – more comprehensively than anything I have ever read lies in a book about powder skiing. In Deep Powder Snow: 40 Years of Ecstatic Skiing, Avalanches and Earth Wisdom, the late powder skiing pioneer and deep ecology philosopher Dolores LaChapelle uncovered a pattern to the flow/bliss continuum that may be experienced when skiing in powder, and which can be applied with equal effectiveness to whitewater paddling.

Described as the 'round dance of appropriation', an idea initially coined by the philosopher Martin Heidegger, it is an interrelationship between the four elements of earth, sky, gods and mortals. When these four elements are in harmony with one another, humans may experience this profound sense of flow. For 'earth' in the context of skiing read 'mountain', and in the context of canoeing read 'the gradient of the land upon which the river flows'. For 'sky' read 'snow' for skiing and '(snowmelt/rain) water' for canoeing – generally precipitation. The notion of 'gods' is a little more complex to describe, but it centres upon those moments within the natural world when you are aware of the aliveness of all that is around you in its fragile, impermanent, fleeting, undisturbed poise – an awareness which comes from moving lightly, silently and reverently through the world.

Dolores LaChapelle's description of this interplay of the four elements when applied to the movement of skiing in powder is put so beautifully when she wrote[212]

On a clear winter morning, just as the sun rises high enough for its slanting rays to shine horizontally through the trees, disclosing each branch and needle, backlit and rimmed with fire, each intricate facet of the snow crystals, distinct and glittering with many-coloured lights, each contour and dip of the land plainly outlined by the conforming snow, and every animal track sharp and clear, silently I lay my track through the snow – a silent listener awaiting Being. And Being responds. Because of the skis, I move so silently and swiftly that deer, rabbits, and weasels are surprised and caught in their inner lives; so swiftly and silently that they do not flee but stand out in their being. Each tree-being, aspen and fir, lit from within, stands out. The shape of the land is shown forth more clearly than in summer, when its contours are masked and hidden by vegetation. The sky is bluer, more compelling against the contrasting white snow. The earth more present, the sky more present, I, the mortal, more present in total awareness, and thus these three of Heidegger's fourfold are completed by the almost tangible presence of the gods.

The dance of appropriation does not take place as soon as you step out of your car and into a canoe. It takes time to tune into the place where you are, to allow the thoughts buzzing about your head to dissipate or resolve, and to become aware of what is all around you. There is something in portaging a canoe, or skinning up a mountain on skis, that primes you for the dance. Heidegger called this 'breaking open trails' or Bewegung, during which the four elements of earth, sky, the gods and mortals 'acquire a mutual nearness of inter-belonging'.[213] The dance is not something you can pay for in cash and recline waiting to be entertained – it involves, rather, active participation. An active interaction between the elements.

When we talk of an 'active interaction' between the four elements, this requires firstly the canoeist turning him/herself over to gravity and the pattern of water in the river (earth, sky and mortals), and also, as Dolores LaChapelle explained, the mortal having 'a capacity for death'. In the words of Don Juan (as quoted by Dolores LaChapelle): 'The warrior rides with death over his left shoulder.'

This acknowledgement of the possibility of death is significant in that it demonstrates a mortal's humility in the presence of the power of the natural world. In this case, it would be an acknowledgement that 'death is an ever-present possibility' around the world of a river, particularly in rapids and when the river is in spate. There is, therefore, a sense of respect shown by the mortal to the other elements. Also, with death being the transition between the realm of the gods (or 'Being', as Dolores LaChapelle referred to it) and the world of mortals, the ever-present possibility of death while canoeing brings the mortal closer to that line of transcendence. Which is not to say that the greater the risk and the more intense the adrenaline, the more lively the dance of appropriation – no, not at all. I am not talking about an 'extreme' adrenaline sport here, which (in my experience) is more about throwing yourself into highly risk-laden situations simply to soak yourself in adrenaline, swell your ego, and shallowly try to convince yourself that you are more powerful than the natural world. The round dance, rather, is about cooperating with the natural world instead of competing – conforming rather than conquering.

Nevertheless, it is often in that crossover moment between colour and whiteness – for example where the dark peaty water turns to white in a rapid, or where the green blue of a wave crashes into surf – that the gods may be encountered. Therein lies the flux and a zone of gigantic energy.

Ancient Scots pines stand at the bend between the narrow passage through Glenferness and the more open country upstream of Daltra. From the lip of the whitewater ahead, duck rise out of the turbulence and take off downstream, as if the rapids themselves have taken flight. The rock garden here takes time to negotiate and there is no obvious channel for the canoe.

A mile or so later I come to the Douglas fir at Dalnaheiglish Wood where the river forms two powerful shoots as it races between the gneiss corridor. I line the first shoot and paddle the second that starts 30 yards later.

The river tightens again on the approach to Ardclach. The

stream is deep and dark, and the current slower. Giant stones stand like sentries two-by-two through this section, awakening the river into squeezes of speed as it passes each pair. One rock resembles a puffin with its white belly set out against the dark water.

I pull ashore and carry the canoe across the haugh to the car park next to the church at Ardclach, ending a long day's paddle through this central section of the river. I had thought about trying to continue on to Randolph's Leap, but it has just gone 4 o'clock. Tea time. Four o'clock is the hour when you find the most accidents taking place in ski resorts. It's when people's blood sugar is at a low from the day's activities. I'm in no rush, anyway, and it means I can savour the next section down to Randolph's Leap more fully and give it my complete concentration.

I return to Ardclach nearly a month later. The past four weeks have been extremely wet and the river running high. Someone once told me that mountaineering was 80% waiting and 20% action. Paddling whitewater can be similar in that you have to wait for the right conditions to present themselves. Were the Findhorn fed by a glacier, you would have steady paddling through the spring and early summer, with little water come the autumn. With the steep, treeless bowls in the Monadhliaths, rain funnels into the river with more intensity than any other catchment I know. Venture out in the wrong conditions when your gut instinct is telling you it's a bad idea, and you have all the makings of an accident waiting to happen.

Back on the water, and the first stretch down to Logie Bridge is slow going. Strainer trees stretching across the river as well as a series of shallow, rock-filled pools mean floating the canoe on a number of occasions. Strainers (where the water pours through the branches) or sweepers (where the fallen tree clears the water) are death traps. They must be avoided at all costs. I once hit a strainer on the upper Spey, but fortunately the canoe capsized in such a way that it shielded me from getting caught on any branches. One technique should you find yourself floating out of your boat and fast approaching a sweeper is to try your hardest to climb up onto the main trunk. Another thing you must always ensure when out paddling is to carry a knife, and if a branch catches your buoyancy aid or part of your clothing you can cut yourself free. As the saying goes, 'Carry a knife, save a life'.

Alder has taken over as the dominant tree once again after the pines and firs of the past few miles. Nests of sand martins pepper the bank.

> Logie Bridge rocks
> Float
> Like icebergs
> Hinting
> Ominously
> That there is more
> Below
> Than meets the eye

The first rapid after the bridge entails a swift drop for the Canadian canoe, followed by a tight angle on its exit. Then long, smooth bends and shingle passages lead the way on through Coulmony. Dippers flit and dart from the moss-covered rocks. To the left lie haugh fields, to the right a steep, high ridge of fir trees.

I think of the story of Huck Finn and how he drifted on down the great Mississippi. A descendent of the Finn folk. Paddling was in the genes.

The river then gathers after a right-hand bend into a dark pool. Steel-coloured stones rise in a quiver at the head of the next rapid, named after these fang-like structures: the Dragon's Teeth.

The rapid runs for about 40 metres in length. The passage is some six feet wide. On the left of the water stands a continuation of the river-sculpted steel rocks. On the right is a slab wall – named by some as the Wall of Death after the shelf that is said to lie beneath the surface and which has trapped paddlers in the past. The descent through the water looks a gradual decline, without any obvious rocks midstream, but the surge of the water is powerful and strong. I think of Sigurd Olsen's words in The Singing Wilderness:

Is there any suspense that quite compares with that moment of commitment when the canoe heads toward the lip of a long, roaring rapid and then is taken by its unseen power? At first there is no sense of speed, but suddenly you are part of it, involved in spume and spouting rocks. Then when there is no longer any choice and a man knows his fate is out of hand, his is a sense of fierce abandonment when all the voyageurs of the past join the rapids in their shouting.[214]

Commitment is paramount when you run a rapid like this. If you choose to proceed, you must do so wholeheartedly. Any doubt and hesitation, and it's an early bath. At Strathcona Park Lodge in British Columbia I was taught the philosophy of 'The Happy Warrior'. With its roots in Buddhism and the poetry of Wordsworth, the Happy Warrior is someone who, once they commit to a task, decides to do all and bear all cheerfully and bravely. The antithesis is someone who complains relentlessly – the type of person you never want to find yourself with on a wilderness trip. 'There are two types of people,' our instructor at Strathcona, the celebrated climber Rob Wood, told us, 'whiners and bitchers, and Happy Warriors.' One of the noblest acts someone can do, however, once they realise that to proceed is either foolish or dangerous, is to retreat. Applied in the outdoors, and retreat from a bad scene may be your only insurance policy to living a long, healthy life: deciding not to go for the summit when close to the top; choosing to portage a rapid; or opting to avoid that avalanche-loaded slope despite the bounteous powder. As the veteran Himalayan climber Doug Scott once explained, it is often a case of listening to your gut reaction, to that 'little voice within' which is the sum of your experience.

Paddling back up into the dark pool above the rapid, I then line up the 'V'. The canoe is sucked into the channel, topping and tailing the white waves as I brace for stability and paddle frenetically to continue momentum. Spray washes into and over the canoe as I tumble into the foot of the rapid, letting out ecstatic whoops, half-swamped though still afloat.

Paddling to shore I then empty the canoe of water, laughing at the dance I have just been part of, and grateful that the canoe did not flip. Pulse racing. Rapid breathing. Dry throat. Huge smile.

Yet in the frenzy of the roar of the water there were moments of intense serenity, if that seems possible. In the split-second before the smooth water curled up into each white wave there were spaces in which time seemed to bend. Fractions of time felt infinite, with every movement lived in slow motion. As if alertness opened the door into a new dimension. Eyes skimmed. Total focus. Paddling into the white.

Rounding the next bend a heron and buzzard scrap it out, writhing in mid-air above the old Scots pines. I can't make out what they are fighting over. Neither bird is grasping any food. It could be a question of territorial air space.

The river feels deep here as it ghosts its way on in a slow and steady rhythm.

The approach to Daltulich Bridge is marked by a rapid known by many paddlers as Carnage Corner. There is a short, two-stage drop, down which the water squeezes its full river-width into a narrow path. In the middle of the channel is a jagged fin of rock awaiting any unsuspecting paddler.

After a lengthy scout of the rapid I opt to portage, before drifting on under the bridge and over a rock the shape of a crocodile's head. The river then shuggles its way through a swift left-right shoot, before entering the long avenue to Randolph's Leap.

We are now back in the realm of the mighty Douglas firs. It feels serene to descend through this straight of mini chutes and deep pools. There is a weight to the land – an ancient quality – that you sense even from the water. Maybe it's the calm before the storm of the whitewater below Randolph's Leap.

As the river sweeps down towards the Leap, I pull into an eddy and exit up the bank of beeches.

CHAPTER TEN

The Sands of Time

'Below high cliffs
all day I see plants
no sign of people
yellow leaves in the wind
birds call at dusk from the valley
the mountain moon rises at night
a crane takes flight from a pine
and showers my robe with dew.'

Stonehouse, 14th-century Chinese hermit[215]

Portaging a canoe down the goat track to the pool at Sluie could
be an Olympic event. After the initial bumpy road, you follow a
path overgrown with slippery grass before performing a limbo
dance under an oak tree. There then comes a hairpin where I
choose to drop the canoe, flipping it onto its hull and lining
it back the other way over a steeper section of mud, rock and
acorns. Next comes the drop where I lower the boat with a rope
as slowly as possible, hoping the canoe will not slip away and
the rope burn my hands. Once the canoe is securely parked on
the strip of beach, there is a precarious leap along the muddy
bank, grasping onto hazel branches for stability. Reunited with
the canoe, I unshoulder my waterproof pack and pretend I'm
not out of breath.

WHITE RIVER

The pool at Sluie is about 70 yards wide but, given the sandstone shelf on the right-hand side of the river, is particularly shallow when you first paddle out. I cross towards the far bank and then head upstream into the tail of the gorge. This is a good place to warm up and stretch out the shoulder muscles. The spouts of whitewater in the pool and the number of eddies formed by isolated gneiss rocks make it an excellent place to practise ferry-gliding the canoe. Ferry-gliding is a way of being able to cross the current without being forced downstream. The secret is being able to position the nose of the boat at the correct angle to the current, and to make micro adjustments as you cross depending on the speed of the water in that particular vector of the river. When you manage to find the correct angle, you feel no resistance in the water to your paddle strokes – it is like paddling in air.

Typically you will start off with the boat pointing upstream in an eddy (there is a more advanced technique called a 'backward ferry' where you face downstream). Where the downstream flow borders the upstream movement of the water in an eddy, this is known as the eddy line. To get out of the eddy and across the eddy line, you need three things – speed, angle and a lean downstream. With speed you can punch across the flux of the eddy line, and with a downstream lean – in other words you present some of the hull upstream – you should avoid being capsized. As for the angle, it can help to imagine the face of a clock, and if the nose of the canoe was pointing directly upstream this would be 12 o'clock. If you were starting on the left-hand side of the river looking upstream (which confusingly would be river right) and the current was quite fast, you might start off by angling the bow of the canoe to 1 o'clock. As you traverse the river, maintaining a steady forward stroke and ruddering or sweeping as need be to maintain your angle, you may find that the current is less strong on the far side of the water, and in which case you can afford to open the angle of the canoe to 2 o'clock. Coming back the other way, you might start off at 10 o'clock and tighten your angle to 11 o'clock as the current quickens. When you cross the eddy line on the far side of the river, you need to make sure you lean in the opposite direction, in other words upstream, so that you don't capsize. The principle as I try to think of it is essentially that the faster the water, the closer to 12 o'clock you need to be. Also, by harnessing the ever-changing flow of the river as effectively as possible, you minimise the amount of effort you need to exert.

Turning in the pool known as the Whirling Hurl, I notice a series of white veins of rock zig-zagging along the grey corridor of gneiss. The canoe slips into the current as I move at the same speed as the leaves that have already fallen, now riding on the water down to the sea.

> Autumn is
> Already here
> With geese
> Snaking
> South
> Through the skies
> And the belly dancer
> Coins
> Of aspen
> Jangling
> In the wind

The pool at Sluie marks the transition from the gneiss section of river to Old Red Sandstone. The rapid across this geological shift at the tail of the Sluie pool is a tight left-hand bend. It may not look like much but it's full of surprises. There are the two rocks you have to slip through mid-stream, as if passing between the Symplagades. Smaller rocks may run you aground here in the fast current, or sweep you broadside onto one of the bigger rocks. After the sharp turn to the left you have to cross far enough over to avoid an underwater column of sandstone, which in any event forms a standing wave that runs at 45 degrees to the water's surface. It's a fun rapid to run in the right height of water. A friend and I once swamped here in the standing wave one December day, having thought we were home and dry after the rocks at the head of the rapid – and it was a day when the black snow melt ran freshly chilled from the Monadhliaths.

Thomas Henderson wrote about the 'three or four terrific clefts in the solid rock, only three or four feet in width'[216] in the bed of the river here that reach down to 'unknown depths'. These are known as 'The Cracks'. God only knows how far down these fissures plummet, but the sensation of being suspended by the water above these deep realms yet floating through a canyon of sky-climbing sandstone cliffs is an other-worldly experience. Whenever I paddle this section, through the massive towers of sandstone, it feels as if I am travelling through aboriginal lands. Sacred ground. But then again, the entire river is sacred. The whole natural world is sacred. It's just that I'm now back in the area of the river that I know best, the part closest to where I grew up. The place in the natural world that I feel most connected to, that I am part of, and which is part of me.

The idea that a human can feel that they form a part of the river and the river a part of them may seem to some as being a little woo-woo, hocus pocus, and mumbo jumbo. Western philosophy, science and religion have had the effect of casting fact through repetition that we are but atomised individuals, that our egos are the centre of the universe, and that the world was created for humans to lounge about in and to slash, hack and gobble up if we so please. For those that remain in such a dislocated realm, cut off from feeling the reciprocity between self and the natural world, I can only encourage them to venture out more.

What I am beginning to sense is that consciousness is infinite. Looking back at how trapped inside the glass bottle of my own ego I used to be (to paraphrase D.H. Lawrence) for many years – bordered by starched convention, netted by unchallenged assumptions, hopelessly floundering in a twilight existence – I thought of consciousness as micro-cosmic. I never knew that life could be genuinely experienced outside of the confines of the self. For me, it became a question of moving beyond the mental noise of the ego, and step by step experiencing the world anew. It is only by quieting the ego that we may have the awareness to experience the world more deeply, more groundedly and more colourfully.

It was the poem Labrador by Kenneth White that summed up much of this outward, expansive, exploratory movement to me most coherently.[217]

> I lived and moved
> as I had never done before
> became a little more than human even
> knew a larger identity
>
> the tracks of caribou in the snow
> the flying of wild geese
> the red autumn of the maple tree

bitten by frost.
all these became more real to me,
more really me
than my very name

I found myself saying things like
'at one with the spirit of the land'
but there was no 'spirit', none
that was outworn language
and this was a new world,
and my mind was, almost, a new mind.

Labrador captures those first footsteps into a transpersonal world. It captures, for me, what living in an age beyond rampant industrial growth and collateral environmental damage is all about. To move away from the confusion and misdirection of the modern world into a new space beyond neurotic frenzy. This space that can be found when we connect with the larger non-human world. We may say that 'it's a small world' – and indeed we humans are doing our bit to make it smaller by trashing old growth temperate and rain forests, depleting fish stocks to extinction, and poisoning rivers with chemicals in the name of progress and with weapons in the name of peace – and it is small if you travel by jet plane or experience the natural environment solely from the frontier of your armchair. Start travelling on the Earth by foot, by canoe, by horse, by ski – silently – measuring out the true space of the planet we inhabit, and you may just find that there is more to consciousness than the constructs of the human intellect.

The Australian eco-philosopher Warwick Fox has mapped this progressive interface between psychology and ecology more succinctly than anyone so far. In his book Toward a Transpersonal Ecology: Developing New Foundations for Environmentalism,[218] Fox explores three ways in which humans can identify more closely with the natural world and thus acknowledge that we are part of something far grander and more complex than our narcissistic selves. These three forms are defined as personally based identification, ontologically based identification, and cosmologically based identification.

Personally based identification exists when we simply build a relationship with an aspect of the natural world, by watching its actions and its changes and interacting in some capacity over a period of time. You may, for example, watch a particular bird feed at your bird table throughout the year. The bird's presence becomes part of your day and you are all the happier to see it around; similarly, the bird benefits when you leave food on a bird table. Ontologically based identification takes place when you acknowledge that the natural world is there – right there – that its existence cannot be ignored, and that it is not all void, empty and bland. It may be a stunning mountain landscape, being in the presence of a giant tree, or an encounter with wildlife that is a particularly memorable and profound experience that strengthens this type of identification – and my experience is that the more time I spend in wild places, the more unshakeable my respect for the natural world becomes. Finally we come to the cosmologically based identification, which Fox describes as the realisation 'that we and all other entities are aspects of a single unfolding reality'.[219] Essentially this means having a grasp of the theory of evolution, and realising that all life is part of an ongoing, interconnected dance.

So to the sandstone cliffs through which this river flows.

WHITE RIVER

I've watched the colours
Of the stone
Change in the light
And in the weather
From every shade
Of honey
Cream
Pink and ochre

Seen the aspen
Shiver to saffron
The bloodening
Of the rowan
And the bronzing
Of the bracken
Beneath the violet skies
Of autumn

Shivered at delicious
Dark
Deep water channels
Funnelling
Through shelves
And ledges
At the branches of light
Projected from ripples
Onto buttress walls

Felt but transitory
In the steeped
Experience

THE SANDS OF TIME

Of compressions
Folds
And waves of rock

Yet for each moment
Each passing moment
Part of the picture
Witnessing
The changes
Outwith and within

I come ashore at the island in the Soldier's Hole to line the canoe down the right channel. Whereas the left channel carries more water and seems the obvious line to take, you soon discover that its swift tail is loaded with boulders. I've tried to paddle this left channel before, succumbing to its siren calling rumble, and on each occasion the canoe flipped. Maybe a few winter spates will open a channel in time to come. As I head off down the right side I watch a herring gull float the prelude to the left channel as it nonchalantly bobs downriver. Will it run the rapid, I think to myself? And moments later, just before the first waves of whitewater, it paddles its wings and coasts through the air over the set of rapids, touching down in the deep water beyond the boulders. There is just enough water to slip the canoe through the right channel beneath the cliffs. At the downstream end of the island I look up at the rapids guarding the tail of the left channel I avoided, and am glad I didn't try this route as there is still no way through.

Drifting on down amongst the oak woods of Darnaway and Altyre it feels good to pass the trees, cliffs and bends in the river I have known all my life. To be back in the land of the familiar.

WHITE RIVER

The place where I am native. This journey has opened my senses to a wider thread that runs between everything in the watershed. I feel closer, too, to the place where I dwell, as if spending time beyond human company has deepened a developing dialogue with the natural world. Beginning to learn the language of place extends the way in which we relate to other places in the world, almost creating and strengthening the context in which to live and from which to move outwards. The closer we grow towards the natural environment of a place, learning its intricacies and moods and fragilities, the more likely we are to dwell more carefully and live with greater stability in the realms of the ecological and the psychological.

Around the rapid at St John's before the days of bridges across the river, there used to be a ferry. The character of the ferryman in Hermann Hesse's Siddhartha comes to mind, and his wise words that much can be learned from a river.[220]

Lessons in respecting
The unrelenting power
Of water

Fleeting moments
Ensconced
In untamed beauty

The unfailing search
To follow the right way
Whatever the obstacles

That turbulence
Is always followed

THE SANDS OF TIME

By calm
Somewhere around the bend

That rivers
Do not judge
But accept
And move on

That there is neither beginning
Nor end
Merely resolutions

That all is connected

The alder trees thicken again on the approach to Mundole. Passing under the road bridge for the A96 and then the railway bridge, the surroundings feel so very different from the wild country upstream. Yet this is the same river, connecting the variety of habitats, species, landscapes, dwellings and human activities. The same river that gathers its first drops of water above the peat hags of the Monadhliaths, sings through the barren lands of the Streens, thunders and sighs through the forest gorges, and now races seawards beneath the gulls.

Amidst this mix of places, wildlife and people you realise that despite all the differences we are all bound by the same thread. The river does indeed run through us all. Downstream influences upstream. Upstream influences downstream.

Tight s-bends shape their way through gravel beds as the river winds its way through the Laich fields past Forres. In the run-out bayou of the river lie half-submerged willow and birch trees washed downstream in spates. Gannets perch on their branches and mark an entry to the tidal zone. The air smells of salt. In the wide body of water of the bay the land seems but a sliver between sky and sea.

Moving out over the clear water towards the fringes of the Culbin around Binsness, the village of Findhorn tucked in along the far shore, I think of that vast expanse of wave and sky beyond the coast, which Henry Thoreau once called a 'wilderness reaching round the globe, wilder than a Bengal jungle'.[221] Yet so much marine life from whales to cod to coral reefs to the anadromous salmon has been threatened to critical levels, forming an alarming trend that must stop. It seems hard to believe that humans could have set in motion and continue to stoke an economic machine that runs on the Earth's natural capital, and continue to pontificate about its prowess whilst bullying and threatening and mocking anyone who tries to stand in its way. This is the reality and the misplaced concreteness of international politics and economics. Just how long this unsustainable march can continue is unclear, before either the effects of climate change reach their most devastating and biodiversity collapses, or before governments reach levels of such fixated craving for wealth that they declare war on all who stand in their path.

We do not need to go down this route.

We already have all the tools available to live abundantly and with greater harmony on the Earth. From the design principles of energy efficient buildings and eco-friendly vehicles, to the application of appropriately located forms of renewable energy. From the food production patterns and philosophies of permaculture and organic agriculture, to the political structures of bioregionalism. From the creative lifeforce of ecological restoration, to the business theories of natural capitalism. These ideas are tried and tested. They work and they each have the potential to trigger further creativity and stability. It is simply a matter of action.

It is not without coincidence that the symbol of wisdom in ancient Celtic culture was the salmon, as we need wisdom now more than ever. In times of disorientation when links to the variety of human connections to the planet have been largely extinguished by a global monoculture, we need to listen to the river once again – to the mountains, the forests, the fields, shores and oceans – to rediscover these lessons. We need the songs to share the experience so that we might pass the guidelines on to future generations. An abundant return of wild salmon could be a beacon on this new path away from misdirection. Wild salmon recovery requires humanity to relinquish unsustainable practices and help create more vibrant habitats. Working to bring back the return of wild salmon could introduce society to an older yet contemporary rhythm, to a deeper understanding that everything is connected, and to a more balanced and colourful way of living closer to the Earth.

Rainclouds are moving in from the Knock of Braemoray. As I paddle out towards the firth an oyster catcher weaves between the troughs of green waves. I land the canoe on the shore below the steep dunes beneath the pines and walk to the headland where I began this journey.

> The sky to the North
> Stretches out
> In a camouflage of blues

WHITE RIVER

The surf
Around high tide
Pounds into the shore
Retreating back to sea
Over the chorus
Of mountain stones

Windy Bay, Haida Gwaii

'All the wilderness was quickened,
Everywhere the woods were greening,
Trees were leafing, grass was growing,
Birds were singing, thrushes warbling –
Over all a cuckoo calling.
Berry bushes grew abundant,
Golden flowers filled the meadow.'

The Kalevala[222]

Some time after, I travelled beyond the watershed of the River Findhorn to a place far away. Across the North Atlantic and the tundra barrens of Canada, beyond the forested coasts of British Columbia and over the often furious Hecate Strait, lies Haida Gwaii – otherwise known as the Queen Charlotte Islands.

On a flat-calm ocean, I paddled into Windy Bay in my sea kayak and stayed there for a night, resting in the longhouse of the Haida people.

Like much of Haida Gwaii (at least the parts that have escaped and are now protected from commercial logging), the greens of the forest canopy and the mosses and grasses of the forest floor were some of the purest greens imaginable – as green as the emerald villages of Ladakh and the tropical myriad of Tahiti. The trees themselves were enormous, with one giant Sitka thought to be over 2,000 years old.

WHITE RIVER

It was the time of year when the pink salmon run, and they filled the bay in their thousands, waiting for the tide to rise to help carry them upstream some distance into the spawning beds deep inside the cedar forest. Black bears stalked the burns, seals patrolled the bay, and bald eagles and ravens perched in the wings of this dynamic stage awaiting their moment.

In this place of pulsating ecology, in this abundant rhythm, I lay at night in the longhouse with a calmness only ever experienced when by the River Findhorn. Like some familiar dream, this felt intimate ground from some other time.

The peace and abundance were no fantasy, but a complete possibility and reality. Indeed, the natural vibrancy and cultural richness of Haida Gwaii create colossal hope for the future of the River Findhorn and for the environmental state of the greater Atlantic region, which we can help restore to full health and diversity.

There is good work to be done and songs to be sung of the bounty that surrounds us.

Notes

1. Watts, Alan W. 'On The Tantra', in Mademoiselle magazine, July 1967.
2. Phoca vitulina, L. Common Seal. In A Vertebrate Fauna of The Moray Basin, Vol. 1, David Douglas, Edinburgh, 1895, p. 184, Harvie-Brown, J.A and Buckley, T.E. write: 'Seals are still abundant along the shores and at the bars and mouths of rivers, especially the Findhorn, Spey, and Deveron, but they are not so plentiful nor so destructive as the "forests" of stake- and bag-nets which range for miles along the coast-line.'
3. MacAulay, John M. Seal-Folk and Ocean Paddlers (Sliochd nan Ron), The White Horse Press, Cambridge and the Isle of Harris, 1998, pp. 33–34. Reference to MacFarlane, A.M. 'Sea Myths of the Hebrides', Transactions of the Inverness Scientific Society and Field Club, 1918–25, Vol. 9, pp. 360–390.
4. MacGregor, A.A. The Peat Fire Flame, 1937. Quoted in MacAulay, John M. Seal-Folk and Ocean Paddlers as above at p. 15.
5. Thomas, Captain Frederick W.L. Proceedings of the Society of Antiquaries of Scotland, 1867, VII, pp. 193–4. Quoted in MacAulay, John M. Seal-Folk and Ocean Paddlers, as above at pp. 23–25.
6. Levi-Strauss, Claude Tristes Tropiques, Penguin Books, 1992, pp. 255–256. Translated from the French by Weightman, John and Doreen. First published by Librarie Plon, 1955.
7. Hecateus of Abdera, a pupil of Pyrrho the Sceptic and a philosopher at the court of Ptolemy. 4th Century BC Greece. Sourced from White, Kenneth 'The Archaic Context', in On Scottish Ground: Selected Essays, Polygon, Edinburgh, 1998, p. 27. Hecateus described the indigenous people of Britain as 'Hyperborean', meaning that they lived 'beyond the North wind'.

8. Nietzsche, Frederick The Will to Power, Random House Inc., New York. Vintage Books Edition, 1968.

9. Gauguin, Paul D'ou venons-nous? Que sommes-nous? Ou allons-nous? (Where are we from? What are we? Where are we going?). Painted in Tahiti, French Polynesia, 1897. Tompkins Collection, Museum of Fine Arts, Boston.

10. Muir, John My First Summer in the Sierra, Diadem, London and The Mountaineers, Seattle. In John Muir: The Eight Wilderness-Discovery Books, 1992, p. 248. First published in 1910.

11. Chatwin, Bruce The Songlines, Vintage, 1998, pp. 13–14.

12. Sutherland, Elizabeth In Search of the Picts: A Celtic Dark Age Nation, Constable, 1994, pp. 1–3.

13. Cummins, W.A. The Picts and their Symbols, Sutton Publishing, 1999, p. 35. This stone is now in the National Museum of Antiquities.

14. Rutherford, Ward Celtic Lore, Aquarian/Thorsons, 1993.

15. See Sutherland, Elizabeth In Search of the Picts: A Celtic Dark Age Nation above, pp. 5–6. Reprinted with kind permission of the author.

16. Abram, David The Spell of the Sensuous: Perception and Language in a More-Than-Human World, Vintage Books, 1996, p. 7.

17. Sherley-Price L. (trs.) Bede: Ecclesiastical History of the English People with Bede's Letter to Egbert and Cuthbert's Letter on the Death of Bede, Revised edition, Harmondsworth, Penguin, 1990, p. 46. Sourced from Cummins, W.A. The Age of the Picts, Sutton, 1995. According to Bede, the Picts sailed from Scythia arriving firstly on the north coast of Ireland where they had been blown by storms. The Irish would not allow the Picts to settle in Ireland and suggested instead that they head to the northern part of Britain. The Picts were, however, granted wives by the Irish on the condition that, as Bede wrote, 'when any dispute arose, they should choose a king from the female line rather than the male' – a custom that continued among the Picts.

18. Eliade, Mircea Shamanism: Archaic Techniques of Ecstasy, Princeton University Press – Bollingen Series, 1964, pp. 394–396; citation of Herodotus quoted here, with reference to Godley A.D., tr. Herodotus. London and New York, 1921–24, (Loeb Classical Library). 4 volumes.

NOTES

19. Rampini, Sheriff A History of Moray and Nairn, p. 6.
20. White, Kenneth 'The Archaic Context' in On Scottish Ground: Selected Essays, Polygon, Edinburgh, 1998, pp. 24–25.
21. Smyth, Alfred P. Warlords and Holy Men: Scotland AD 80–1000, Edinburgh University Press, 1984. See Chapter 3, 'The Last Men on Earth, the Last of the Free', p. 45.
22. Rampini, Sheriff A History of Moray and Nairn, p. 13. Sheriff Rampini described the Picts as follows: 'They were inured to fatigue, hunger, and cold. They would run into the morasses up to the neck. They could live for days in their desolate wastes without any other food than roots or leaves. They were armed with bucklers, poniards, and lances with metal balls attached to their lower ends, which they shook to frighten their enemies; and they fought from chariots.'
23. Newton, Michael A Handbook of the Scottish Gaelic World, Four Courts Press, Dublin, 2000, p. 45.
24. See Rampini above, p. 25.
25. See Rampini above, pp. 25–34.
26. Ross, Sinclair The Culbin Sands – Fact or Fiction, Centre for Scottish Studies, University of Aberdeen, 1992. See Chapter 4, 'Recent and Contemporary Change'; also, Findhorn Village Heritage Company, 'The Culbin Sands'.
27. Findhorn Village Heritage Company, 'The Lost Villages of Findhorn'.
28. Henderson, Thomas The Findhorn: The River of Beauty, Grant & Murray, Edinburgh, 1932, p. 21.
29. Cook, Martin Birds of Moray and Nairn, The Mercat Press, Edinburgh, 1992, pp. 82–83.
30. Personal conversation with Roy Dennis, wildlife expert and consultant. Roy has been the leading catalyst for the reintroduction of ospreys, sea eagles and red kites to Scotland.
31. Gibran, Kahlil 'The King Hermit', in The Forerunner: His Parables and Poems, Heinemann, London, 1974, p. 11. First published in 1963.
32. Shelton, Richard and Heath, Sarah (eds) Biennial Review 1999–2001 of FRS Freshwater Laboratory, Faskally, Perthshire. Scottish Executive Rural Affairs Department, pp. 4, 6, 12 and 13.
33. Lauder, Sir Thomas Dick The Great Floods of August, 1829, in the

Province of Moray and Adjoining Districts. Reprinted by Moray Books, Forres in 1998. See Chapters 8 and 9.

34. Lauder, Sir Thomas Dick The Great Floods of August, 1829, in the Province of Moray and Adjoining Districts. Reprinted by Moray Books, Forres in 1998. Poem cited on page 75. The Divie and Dorback are two of the main tributaries of the Findhorn, draining the north-east side of the Dava Moor and joining the River Findhorn at Relugas.

35. Basho, Matsuo The Narrow Road to the Deep North and Other Travel Sketches, Penguin Classics, 1966, p. 97.

36. Lawrence, D.H. 'The Escape', from The Complete Poems of D.H. Lawrence, Viking Penguin, 1971.

37. Nash, Roderick Wilderness and the American Mind, Yale University Press, 1982, p. 3.

38. Leopold, Aldo 'The Wilderness and its Place in Forest Recreational Policy', Journal of Forestry, 1921, 19, p. 719.

39. Marshall, Robert 'The Problem of the Wilderness', Scientific Monthly, 1930, 30, p. 141.

40. US Wilderness Act, section 2(c).

41. Nash, Roderick Wilderness and the American Mind, Yale University Press, 1982, p. 3.

42. Service, Robert 'The Call of the Wild'. Collected Poems of Robert Service, G. P. Putnam's Sons, New York, 1907, p.17

43. Graham, John 43. Outdoor Leadership: Technique, Common Sense and Self-Confidence, The Mountaineers, Seattle, 1997, p. 12.

44. Thoreau, Henry David Walden, The Modern Library, New York, 1992, p. 86.

45. Dwelly, Edward The Illustrated Gaelic-English Dictionary, Gairm Publications, Glasgow, 1994.

46. Bain, George The River Findhorn: From Source to Sea, Nairnshire Telegraph Office, 1911, p. 135.

47. Watson, W.J. History of the Celtic Place-names of Scotland, (1926–1930). Sourced from M.T.T. Phillips 'The History of the Ancient Oak Forest of Darnaway and its Timber', Paper submitted for publication to Scottish Forestry, October 1998.

48. Anon. The Royal Scottish Arboricultural Society 4th Annual Excursion, August 1881. Source provided by M.T.T. Phillips in 'The History of the Ancient Oak Forest of Darnaway and its Timber' – see above.

NOTES

49. Stell, G. and Baillie, M. The Great Hall and Roof of Darnaway Castle, 1987. Report presented to Moray Estates. Source provided by M.T.T. Phillips – see above.

50. Henderson, Thomas The Findhorn: The River of Beauty, Grant & Murray, Edinburgh.

51. Anderson, M.L. A History of Scottish Forestry, Nelson, Edinburgh and London, 1967. Source provided by M.T.T. Phillips – see above.

52. Shaw, Revd. L. The Natural History of Moray, Wm Auld, Edinburgh, 1774. Source provided by M.T.T. Phillips – see above.

53. Anderson, M.L. A History of Scottish Forestry, Nelson, Edinburgh and London, 1967. Source provided by M.T.T. Phillips – see above.

54. Stell, G. and Baillie, M. The Great Hall and Roof of Darnaway Castle, 1987. Report presented to Moray Estates. Source provided by M.T.T. Phillips – see above.

55. Shaw, Revd. L. The Natural History of Moray, Wm Auld, Edinburgh, 1774. Source provided by M.T.T. Phillips – see above.

56. Scott, D. Report of Darnaway Forest and Neighbouring Woods, 1912. Unpublished report in Darnaway Estate Papers. Source provided by M.T.T. Phillips – see above.

57. Phillips, M.T.T. 'The History of the Ancient Oak Forest of Darnaway and its Timber', Paper submitted for publication to Scottish Forestry, October 1998.

58. Ursos arctos. Archibald Thorburn in Thorburn's Mammals, Book Club Associates, 1974. First published in 1920–21 in British Mammals.

59. Semeniuk, Robert 'Do Bears Fish in the Woods', The Ecologist, Dec 2001/Jan 2002, 31(10), pp. 32–35. The article reports on the research of Professor Tom Reimchen, biologist and holistic evolutionary geneticist, of the University of Victoria, British Columbia. Professor Reimchen specialises in predator–prey interactions. The article describes the ecological relationships between salmon, bears and trees as follows (p. 33): 'Reimchen estimates that 70 per cent of a bear's annual protein comes from salmon, and that during the 45 days of the spawn each black bear catches about 700 fish and leaves half of each carcass in the forest. At 2.2kg per fish, this amounts to 120kg of nitrogen fertiliser per hectare of land. British Columbia's 80,000 to 120,000 bears could be transferring 60 million kg of salmon tissue into the rainforest,

accounting for half of the nitrogen fixed by some old growth trees.'

60. Lauder, Sir Thomas Dick The Great Moray Floods of 1829, Moray Books, 1998, p. 73.

61. Henderson, Thomas The Findhorn: The River of Beauty, Grant & Murray, Edinburgh, 1932, p. 201. See also, Sobieski, John 'The Templar's Tomb', in Lays of the Deer Forest, Vol. 1, William Blackwood and Sons, Edinburgh and London, and Charles Dolman, London, 1848, pp. 1–99.

62. St. John, Charles Wild Sports and Natural History of the Highlands, Gurney and Jackson, London and Edinburgh, 1927, p. 307.

63. Matheson, Donald Place Names of Elginshire, Eneas McKay, Stirling, 1905.

64. Henderson, Thomas The Findhorn: The River of Beauty, Grant & Murray, Edinburgh, 1932, p. 103.

65. Paper written by Mr Fraser Henderson who once lived at Sluie: 'Sluie: The Place of the Spear', and kindly provided to me by Tony and Alison Brown.

66. Henderson, Thomas The Findhorn: The River of Beauty, Grant & Murray, Edinburgh, 1932, pp. 79–80.

67. McDonough, William and Braungert, Michael Cradle To Cradle: Remaking The Way We Make Things, North Point Press, March 2002.

68. See for example the magazine of the organisation Reforesting Scotland.

69. Paper written by Mr Henderson who once lived at Sluie: 'Sluie: The Place of the Spear'. The paper was kindly provided to me by Tony and Alison Brown.

70. Gunn, Neil Highland River, Faber & Faber, 1937, pp. 34–35. Reprinted with kind permission of Dairmid Gunn and the Neil Gunn Literary Estate.

71. Bain, George The River Findhorn: From Source to Sea, Nairnshire Telegraph Office, 1911, p. 139.

72. See Hart, Cyril and Raymond, Charles British Trees in Colour, Book Club Associates, London, 1973.

73. MacLean, Norman A River Runs Through It, University of Chicago Press, 1976, p. 1.

74. St. John, Charles Natural History and Sport in Moray, David Douglas, Edinburgh, 1882, pp. 221–222.

NOTES

75. Hemingway, Ernest 'Big Two-Hearted River', in Lawrence, H. Lea A Hemingway Odyssey: Special Places in his Life, Cumberland House Publishing, Nashville, Tennessee.

76. Shelton, Richard and Heath, Sarah (eds) Biennial Review 1999–2001 of FRS Freshwater Laboratory, Faskally, Perthshire. Scottish Executive Rural Affairs Department, pp. 4, 6, 12, 13. See also: The Nature of Scotland: A Policy Statement.

77. See The Atlantic Salmon Trust's website at: www. atlanticsalmontrust.org

78. All information supplied here, unless stated otherwise, comes from: World Wide Fund for Nature The Status of Wild Atlantic Salmon: A River by River Assessment, May 2001. www.wwf-uk.org/news/pdfs,atlanticSalmon.pdf (consulted July 2001).

79. These conditions such as 'endangered' and 'critical' are based upon criteria used by the World Conservation Movement (IUCN) in its Red List for species, 2000.

80. Shelton, Richard and Heath, Sarah (eds) Biennial Review 1999–2001 of FRS Freshwater Laboratory, Faskally, Perthshire. Scottish Executive Rural Affairs Department, pp. 4, 6, 12, 13. See also: The Nature of Scotland: A Policy Statement, The Scottish Executive, p. 20, where it reads: 'The alarming decline in salmon catches, in particular multi-sea winter salmon, over a number of years is a symptom of ecological and fisheries management problems.'

81. Information taken from the annual publications of the Statistical Bulletin of the Department of Agriculture and Fisheries between the years 1982 and 2000. I am most grateful to Jane Robins, the Librarian at the Freshwater Fisheries Laboratory at Faskally, for providing me with this data.

82. Personal correspondence with the River Findhorn District Fisheries Board.

83. Forestry Commission: Forests and Water Guidelines, 3rd edn, Forestry Commission, Edinburgh, 2000, p. 7. Also, personal communication with Dr Richard Shelton, formerly of the FRS Freshwater Laboratory, Faskally, Perthshire and now of the University of St. Andrews.

84. Stephen, A.D. 'Interactions between Catchment Afforestation and Salmonid Populations', West Galloway Fisheries Trust, Annual Report, 1996, pp. 5–9.

85. Anon. Forests and Water Guidelines, 3rd edn, Forest Authority, Edinburgh, 1993.

86. Anon. Prevention of Environmental Pollution from Agricultural Activity, The Scottish Office Agriculture, Environment and Fisheries Department, Edinburgh, 1997. Eutrophication is a process whereby excess nutrients in the water (for example, from agricultural fertilisers) stimulate excessive plant growth in the water and reduce dissolved oxygen necessary for fish survival.

87. For a guide to farming and water management plans, see for example WWF Scotland's Wild Rivers Project and publication, 'What's Good for Rivers is Good for People'.

88. Mackay, D.W. 'Perspectives on the Environmental Aspects of Aquaculture', Transcript of a presentation made at Aquaculture Conference, Trondheim, Norway, October 1999. Scottish Environmental Protection Agency.

89. Atlantic Salmon Trust website: www.atlanticsalmontrust.org

90. McLay, A. and Gorden-Rogers, K. Report of Scottish Salmon Strategy Task Force, Scottish Office, Edinburgh, 1997.

91. NASCO Report on ICES Committee on Fisheries Management, CNL (99) 12. NASCO, Edinburgh, 1999.

92. Friedland, K., Hanson, L.P. and Dunkley D.A. 'Marine Temperatures experienced by post-smolts and the survival of Atlantic salmon, Salmo salar L, in the North Sea Area', Fisheries Oceanography, 1998, 7(1), pp. 22–24.

93. Butler, J. Annual Review, 1998–1999, Wester Ross Fisheries Trust, Inverness, 1999.

94. Thompson, P.M., McConnell, B., Tollet, D.J., Mackay, A., Hunter, C. and Racey, P. 'Comparative Distribution and Diet of Harbour and Grey Seals from the Moray Firth, NE Scotland', Journal of Applied Ecology, 1996, 33, pp. 1572–1584.

95. See Friends of the Earth Scotland website with summary report of The One that Got Away: www.foe-scotland.org.uk/nation/fish_report_summary.html (consulted July 2001).

96. MacGarvin, Malcolm and Jones, Sarah 'Choose or Lose – A Recovery Plan for Fish Stocks and the UK Fishing Industry', 2000, WWF, UK. See website: www.wwf-uk.org/news/pdfs/chooselose.pdf (consulted July 2001).

97. Lauder, Sir Thomas Dick Highland Legends, Hamilton, Adams &

NOTES

Co, London, and Thomas D. Morison, Glasgow, 1880, p. 67.

98. Webster, Mary McCallum Flora of Moray, Nairn & East Inverness, Aberdeen University Press, 1978.

99. Henderson, Thomas The Findhorn: The River of Beauty, Grant & Murray, 1932, pp. 68–69.

100. Bain, George The River Findhorn: From Source to Sea, Nairnshire Telegraph Office, 1911.

101. Korten, David C. 'The Mythic Victory of Market Capitalism', in Mander, Jerry and Goldsmith, Edward (eds) The Case Against the Global Economy, Sierra Club Books, 1996, p. 187.

102. The first four bullet points come from Korten, David C. 'The Mythic Victory of Market Capitalism', in Mander, Jerry and Goldsmith, Edward (eds) The Case Against the Global Economy and For a Turn Toward the Local, Sierra Club Books, San Francisco, 1996, p. 185. The next three bullet points come from Hawken, Paul, Lovins, Amory and Lovins, L. Hunter Natural Capitalism: Creating the Next Industrial Revolution, Little, Brown and Company, Boston, New York and London, 1999, p. 6.

103. Hawken, Paul, Lovins, Amory and Lovins, L. Hunter Natural Capitalism: Creating the Next Industrial Revolution, Little, Brown and Company, Boston, New York and London, 1999, p. 5.

104. Service, Robert 'The Call of the Wild'. Collected Poems of Robert Service, G. P. Putnam's Sons, New York, 1907, p.17

105. Cummins, W.A. The Picts and Their Symbols, Sutton Publishing, Stroud, 1999 p. 35. Gaski, Harald (ed.) Sami Culture in a New Era: The Norwegian Sami Experience, Davvi Girji OS, 1997.

106. Zuckermann, Seth 'Toward a New Salmon Economy', in Salmon Nation: People and Fish at the Edge, An Ecotrust Book, 1999, p. 73.

107. Brower, David Let the Mountains Talk, Let the Rivers Run, New Society Publishers, Gabriola Island, BC, Canada, 2000, Chapter 2: 'Reinventing the Wheels: Hypercars and Neighbourhoods'.

108. WWF Scotland/Scottish Fishermen's Federation, 2000, 'Towards a sustainable fishing industry in Scotland'.

109. Perkins Marsh, George Man and Nature, or Physical Geography as Modified by Human Action, Belknap Press, Harvard University, 1864, pp. 186–188 (2000 edition). See also: Forestry Commision, Edinburgh, 1998, 'Forests and Water Guidelines', 3rd edn.

110. Hawken, Paul, Lovins, Amory and Lovins, L. Hunter Natural Capitalism: Creating the Next Industrial Revolution, Little, Brown and Company, Boston, New York and London, 1999, p. 10.

111. Sale, Kirkpatrick 'Principles of Bioregionalism', in Mander, Jerry and Goldsmith, Edward (eds) The Case Against the Global Economy and For a Turn Toward the Local, Sierra Club Books, San Francisco, 1996, pp. 471–484. Citation from p. 480.

112. Sohm, Debra 'Map of Watershed Restoration Groups Through the Northwest', from Salmon Nation: People and Fish at the Edge, Ecotrust, Portland, Oregon, 1999, p. 66.

113. Zuckerman, Seth 'Toward a New Salmon Economy', from Salmon Nation: People and Fish at the Edge, Ecotrust, Portland, Oregon, 1999, p. 68.

114. Zuckerman, Seth 'Toward a New Salmon Economy', from Salmon Nation: People and Fish at the Edge, Ecotrust, Portland, Oregon, 1999, p. 72.

115. Jernsletten, Nils 'Sami Traditional Terminology: Professional Terms Concerning Salmon, Reindeer and Snow', in Gaski, Harald (ed.) The Norwegian Sami Experience, Davvi Girji OS, Karasjok, Norway, 1997, pp. 95–97.

116. Stone, Christopher Should Trees Have Standing: Toward Legal Rights for Natural Objects, William Kauffman, Inc, 1974. First appeared in the Southern California Law Review, 1972.

117. The first case in Scotland to assert that companies are entitled to human rights was Crummock v HMA – See paragraph 3 of the Opinion of Lord Weir in the Note of Appeal under section 74 of the Criminal Procedure (Scotland) Act 1995, delivered 16 March 2000. This case can be found at the website of the Scottish Courts on www.scotcourts.gov.uk (consulted February 2002).

118. Drever, Helen The Lure of the Kelpie: Fairy and Folk Tales of the Highlands, The Moray Press, Edinburgh & London, 1937, Chapter XI, 'The Cairn of the Lovers: A Tale of the Findhorn', pp. 80–87.

119. Henderson, Thomas The Findhorn: The River of Beauty, Grant & Murray, 1932, p. 68.

120. Henderson, Thomas The Findhorn: The River of Beauty, Grant & Murray, Edinburgh, 1932, pp. 52–53.

NOTES

121. Bain, George The River Findhorn: From Source to Sea, Nairnshire Telegraph Office, 1911, p. 115.

122. Laviolette, Patrick and McIntosh, Alastair 'Fairy Hills: Merging Heritage and Conservation'. First published in ECOS: Journal of the British Association of Nature Conservation, 1997, 18(3/4), pp. 2–8. Also found on www.alastairmcintosh.com/articles/1997_faerie_hills.htm (consulted January 2002).

123. Bain, George The River Findhorn: From Source to Sea, Nairnshire Telegraph Office, 1911, p. 115.

124. Rampini, Charles History of Moray and Nairn, Wm Blackwood & Sons, Edinburgh & London, 1897, p. 67. See also, Mackie, Charles The Wolf, Gopher Publishers, Elgin, Moray, 2001. First published in 1977.

125. Shaw, Lachlan History of the Province of Moray (3 vols), Hamilton, Adams & Co. Ltd. and Thorn. D. Morison, 1882. The name 'Rhiamone' was attributed to The Wolf by his men.

126. Such evidence is straightforward when you look at the woods around Grantown-on-Spey, Dulnain Bridge and Carrbridge. Also see: Watson Featherstone, Alan 'Restoring Scotland's Caledonian Forest', Wild Earth, Fall/Winter 2001–2002, pp. 66–71.

127. Bain, George The River Findhorn: From Source to Sea, Nairnshire Telegraph Office, 1911, p. 50.

128. Lauder, Sir Thomas Dick Highland Legends, Hamilton, Adams & Co, London; Thomas D. Morison, Glasgow, 1880, p. 43.

129. McVean, D.N. and Ratcliffe, D.A. 'Plant Communities of the Scottish Highlands', Monographs of the Nature Conservancy No. 1, 1962.

130. Smout, T.C., MacDonald, Alan R. and Watson, Fiona A History of the Native Woodlands of Scotland 1500–1920, Edinburgh University Press, 2005, p. 11.

131. Anderson, M.L. A History of Scottish Forestry, Nelson, Edinburgh, 1967. Reference sourced from Phillips, Michael T.T. 'Historical Information about the Ancient Forest of Darnaway Estate, Morayshire', Scottish Forestry, 1998, 52(1).

132. McVean, D.N. and Ratcliffe, D.A. 'Plant Communities of the Scottish Highlands', Monographs of the Nature Conservancy No. 1, 1962.

133. Henderson, Thomas The Findhorn: The River of Beauty, Grant & Murray, Edinburgh, 1932, p. 64.

134. Brower, David Let the Mountains Talk, Let the Rivers Run, New Society Publishers, Gabriola Island, BC, Canada, 2000. See Chapter 13. The idea for an Earth Corps extending the remit of the US Peace Corps was proposed by Sam LaBudde.

135. Brower, David Let the Mountains Talk, Let the Rivers Run, New Society Publishers, Gabriola Island, BC, Canada, 2000, pp. 113–114.

136. Brower, David Let the Mountains Talk, Let the Rivers Run, New Society Publishers, Gabriola Island, BC, Canada, 2000, p. 111. David Brower quotes Brigadier Michael Harbottle, OBE, a former senior officer of NATO who stated that: 'The environment probably poses the greatest threat to the survival of the human race.' See also: The Inter-Governmental Panel on Climate Change (IPCC) – the official scientific body established in 1988 by the United Nations to investigate climate change – Second Assessment Report, Summary for Policy Makers, Cambridge University Press, 1995. See also: Bunyard, Peter 'How Global Warming Could Cause Northern Europe to Freeze', in The Ecologist 29(2) – special issue on Climate Change. See also: An Inconvenient Truth presented by Al Gore – Paramount Classics, 2006.

137. Brower, David Let the Mountains Talk, Let the Rivers Run, New Society Publishers, Gabriola Island, BC, Canada, 2000, p. 114.

138. White, Kenneth 'The Archaic Context', in On Scottish Ground: Selected Essays, Polygon, Edinburgh, p. 34.

139. Smout, T.C., MacDonald, Alan R. and Watson, Fiona A History of the Native Woodlands of Scotland 1500–1920, Edinburgh University Press, 2005, p. 122.

140. Bil, A. The Sheiling, 1600–1840, Edinburgh, 1990. Sourced from Smout, T.C., MacDonald, Alan R. and Watson, Fiona A History of the Native Woodlands of Scotland 1500–1920, Edinburgh University Press, 2005.

141. 'Souming' remains the method of regulating livestock on common grazings in the crofting counties today.

142. Smout, T.C., MacDonald, Alan R. and Watson, Fiona A History of the Native Woodlands of Scotland 1500–1920, Edinburgh University Press, 2005, p. 122.

143. Personal communication with gamekeepers from the Lammermuirs and Strathdearn.

144. Bain, George The River Findhorn: From Source to Sea, Nairnshire Telegraph Office, 1911, p. 112.

145. Bain, George The River Findhorn: From Source to Sea, Nairnshire Telegraph Office, 1911, p. 99.

146. Drever, Helen The Lure of the Kelpie: Fairy and Folk Tales of the Highlands, The Moray Press, Edinburgh and London, 1937, Chapter X, 'The Fairy Candles of Pollochaig', p. 76. This reference provides the details for all of this story recounted in these paragraphs.

147. Sobieski, John and Stuart, Charles Edward The Lays of the Deer Forest, William Blackwood & Sons, Edinburgh and London, 1848, Vol. II, pp. 244–247.

148. Leopold, Aldo A Sand County Almanac and Sketches Here and There, Oxford University Press, 1989. First published in 1949. 'Thinking Like a Mountain', p. 129.

149. Leopold, Aldo A Sand County Almanac and Sketches Here and There, Oxford University Press, 1989. First published in 1949. 'Thinking Like a Mountain', pp. 130–131.

150. NAS:GD 50/149 – Moray box Lord Doune no 1/447 – sourced from Smout, T.C., MacDonald, Alan R. and Watson, Fiona A History of the Native Woodlands of Scotland 1500–1920, Edinburgh University Press, 2005, p. 123.

151. Mech, David L. The Wolf: The Ecology and Behaviour of an Endangered Species, University of Minnesota Press, 2000, 10th printing. First published in 1970. See Chapter IX and in particular p. 277. Mech provides a balanced argument in this chapter providing both cases of where wolves do and do not control prey populations. Mech concludes (p. 277) that: 'Wolf predation is the major controlling mortality factor where prey-predator ratios are 24,000 pounds of prey per wolf or less, but at higher ratios wolf predation cannot keep up with annual reproduction.' Scientific studies cited by Mech demonstrating the controlling effects of wolves upon prey populations include: [Deer] Pimlott, D.H. 'Wolf predation and ungulate populations', Amer. Zool., 1967, 7, pp. 267–278; [Dall Sheep] Murie, A. 'The wolves of Mount McKinley', US National Park Service Fauna Series No. 5, 238pp, 1944. Red deer numbers at present in Scotland are at around 350,000 beasts. Biologist Ian Redman of Wolf Help – www.wolfhelp.btinternet.

co.uk/the_wolf_in_scotland.htm – has commented that there are too many red deer in the country for wolves to make an impact upon controlling prey populations. This is in line with Mech's conclusions of 24,000 pounds of prey per wolf being an operative limit. Therefore humans would need to cull deer to controllable numbers first.

152. Leopold, Aldo A Sand County Almanac and Sketches Here and There, Oxford University Press, 1989. First published in 1949. 'Thinking Like a Mountain', p. 130.

153. Staines, B.W. 'The Impact of Red Deer on the Regeneration of Native Pinewoods', Our Pinewood Heritage, Proceedings of a Conference at Inverness, 1994, pp. 107–114. Farnham, Surrey: Forestry Commission, 1995.

154. Darling, Sir Frank Fraser West Highland Survey: An Essay in Human Ecology, Oxford University Press, 1955.

155. Mech, David L. The Wolf: The Ecology and Behaviour of an Endangered Species, University of Minnesota Press, 2000, 10th printing. First published in 1970. See Chapter IX and in particular pp. 278–279.

156. McNamee, Thomas The Return of the Wolf to Yellowstone, Owl Books, Henry Holt and Company, New York, 1997.

157. Holt, Diana 'Should Wolves be Reintroduced to the Highlands of Scotland?', Reforesting Scotland, Summer 2001, 26, pp. 38–40.

158. Mech, David L. The Wolf: The Ecology and Behaviour of an Endangered Species, University of Minnesota Press, 2000, 10th printing. First published in 1970. See Chapter X, p. 291.

159. Rutter, R.J. and Pimlott, D.H The World of the Wolf, JB Lippincott Co., Philadelphia, 1968, p. 202. Rutter and Pimlott reviewed reports of wolf attacks throughout Europe and Asia and concluded that most attacks were probably by rabid wolves.

160. Haglund, Bertil Wolf and Wolverine. Quoted in anonymous 'The Virtuous Wolf', Defenders of Wildlife News, 1967, 42(1), p. 50, in Mech, David L. The Wolf: The Ecology and Behaviour of an Endangered Species, University of Minnesota Press, 2000, 10th printing. First published in 1970. See Chapter X, p. 291.

161. Mech, David L. The Wolf: The Ecology and Behaviour of an Endangered Species, University of Minnesota Press, 2000, 10th printing. First published in 1970. See Chapter X, p. 293.

NOTES

162. Jacobi, Jolande The Psychology of C.G. Jung, Yale University Press, New Haven and London, 1942, pp. 112–113.

163. Clinebell, Howard Ecotherapy – Healing Ourselves, Healing the Earth, The Haworth Press, New York/London, 1996, p. 30.

164. Abram, David The Spell of the Sensuous: Perception and Language in a More-Than-Human World, Vintage Books, 1996. Reprinted with kind permission of Random House Inc.

165. Lopez, Barry Houstun Of Wolves and Men, Touchstone Book, Simon & Schuster, 1995, p. 4.

166. Leopold, Aldo A Sand County Almanac and Sketches Here and There, Oxford University Press, 1989. First published in 1949. 'Thinking Like a Mountain', p. 133.

167. Nilsen, Erlend B. et al. 'Wolf Reintroduction to Scotland: Public Attitudes and Consequences for Red Deer Management', Proceedings of the Royal Society B, 2007, 274, pp. 995–1002. 30 January 2007.

168. St. John, Charles Wild Sports and Natural History of the Highlands, Gurney & Jackson, 1927, p. 47.

169. Leopold, Aldo 'The Upshot', in A Sand County Almanac and Sketches Here and There, Oxford University Press, 1949, pp. 224–225.

170. Erdoes, Richard and Ortiz, Alfonso American Indian Myths and Legends, Pimlico, 1984, pp. 192–193. 'How Mosquitoes Came To Be' [Tlingit].

171. Staines, B.W. 'The Impact of Red Deer on the Regeneration of Native Pinewoods', in Our Pinewood Heritage, Proceedings of a Conference at Inverness, 1994. Forestry Commission, Farnham, Surrey, pp. 107–114.

172. Wigan, Michael The Scottish Highland Estate: Preserving an Environment, Swan Hill Press, Shrewsbury, 1998, p. 42. First published 1991.

173. T Darling, Sir Frank Fraser and Boyd, J. Morton he Highlands and Islands, Fontana New Naturalist, 1964, p. 106.

174. Leopold, Aldo 'Game Methods: The American Way', 1931, in The River of the Mother of God and Other Essays, University of Wisconsin Press, 1991, p. 158.

175. Wheat, Sue 'Cry Wolf', in The Guardian, Wednesday 14 March 2001.

176. Snyder, Gary 'The Wilderness', in Turtle Island, New Directions, New York, 1974, pp. 109–110.

177. Thoreau, Henry David Walden, The Modern Library, New York, 1992 edition, p. 200.

178. Naess, Arne Ecology, Community and Lifestyle, translated and edited by David Rothenberg. Cambridge University Press, 1989, pp. 177–181.

179. Faarlund, Nils A Way Home. Sourced in LaChapelle, Dolores Deep Powder Snow: 40 Years of Ecstatic Skiing, Avalanches and Earth Wisdom, Kivaki Press, 1993, p. 103.

180. Iredale, David Coignafearn, 1998.

181. Mowat, Farley People of the Deer, Michael Joseph, 1952.

182. MacAulay, John M. Seal-Folk and Ocean Paddlers: Sliochd nan Ron, White Horse Press, Cambridge and Harris, 1998, p. 25. John MacAulay writes: 'Adding to the problem surrounding the identity of strangers to our shores, though in another sense it may be a reflection of the same tradition, is the identity of the legendary Fian of Celtic tradition.'

183. White, Kenneth On Scottish Ground: Selected Essays, Chapter 2, 'The Archaic Context'. Polygon, Edinburgh, 1998, pp. 21–22. Reproduced with kind permission of Birlinn Ltd.

184. Bain, George The River Findhorn: From Source to Sea, Nairnshire Telegraph Office, 1911, p. 47.

185. MacAulay, John M. Seal-Folk and Ocean Paddlers: Sliochd nan Ron, White Horse Press, Cambridge and Harris, 1998, p. 22.

186. St. John, Charles Wild Sports and Natural History of the Highlands, Gurney and Jackson, London and Edinburgh, 1927, pp. 290–292 (Chapter XXII).

187. Saigyo Poems of A Mountain Home 1118–1190, translated by Burton Watson Columbia University Press, New York, 1991, p. 174. Reprinted with the kind permission of Columbia University Press.

188. Henderson, Thomas The Findhorn: The River of Beauty, Grant & Murray, Edinburgh, 1932, p. 9.

189. Henderson, Thomas The Findhorn: The River of Beauty, Grant & Murray, Edinburgh, 1932, p. 12

190. Henderson, Thomas The Findhorn: The River of Beauty, Grant & Murray, Edinburgh, 1932, p. 13.

NOTES

191. St. John, Charles Wild Sports and Natural History of the Highlands, Gurney and Jackson, London and Edinburgh, 1927, p. 293 (Chapter XXII). Although St. John does not mention the name of the Cro here, the reference in this passage to Badenoch and Strathspey leans the description in the Cro's favour. Also, George Bain on p. 51 writes that St. John 'struck up the side of the Cro Clach'.

192. Bain, George The River Findhorn: From Source to Sea, Nairnshire Telegraph Office, Nairn, 1911, p. 2.

193. Henderson, Thomas The Findhorn: The River of Beauty, Grant & Murray, Edinburgh, 1932, p. 14.

194. Norberg-Hodge, Helena Ancient Futures: Learning from Ladakh, Sierra Club Books, San Francisco, 1991, pp. 26–30. Here, Helena Norberg-Hodge gives an excellent description of the phu, or summer grazing grounds. I had the chance to experience these pastures in 2000 when I lived with a Ladakhi family on their farm in the mountain village of Hemis Shukpachan, while working on the Ladakh Project – an ecological volunteer programme founded and directed by Helena Norberg-Hodge, and run by the International Society for Ecology and Culture (ISEC).

195. My sincere thanks go to Rob Wood who taught me this principle during a mountaineering expedition on Vancouver Island when I attended the COLT outdoor leadership course at Strathcona Park Lodge. See also Wood, Rob Towards the Unknown Mountains, Ptarmigan Press Ltd, 1991.

196. See: 'River Superintendent Annual Report for Findhorn District Fisheries Board – 1999'.

197. Dogen, 1240, Sansuikyo, 'The Scripture of Mountains and Waters'. Taken from: Cleary, Thomas (translator) Shobogenzo: Zen Essays by Dogen, University of Hawaii Press, Honolulu, 1986.

198. See Henderson, Thomas The Findhorn: The River of Beauty, Grant & Murray, Edinburgh, 1932, p. 13.

199. Holgate, N. 'Palaeozoic and Tertiary Transcurrent Movements in the Great Glen Faul't, Scott. J. Geol., 1969, 5(2), pp. 97–139. Reference taken from: Ross, Sinclair 'The Physical Background', in Omand, David (ed.) The Moray Book, Paul Harris Publishing, Edinburgh, 1976, p. 5.

200. Olson, Sigurd The Singing Wilderness, University of Minnesota Press, 1956, p. 82. Reprinted with kind permission of Robert K. Olson.

201. Robbins, Tom Fierce Invalids Home From Hot Climates, No Exit Press, 2001, p. 39. Reproduced with kind permission of No Exit Press. www.noexit.co.uk

202. Campbell, Joseph The Hero With A Thousand Faces, Bollingen Foundation/Princeton University Press, 1949, p. 92.

203. Original source unknown, but first heard by the author on Ray Mears's series on BBC television about canoeing in Canada.

204. Perkins, Robert Into the Great Solitude: An Arctic Journey, Laurel Expedition/Bantam Doubleday Dell, 1991, p. 3.

205. Rutstrum, Calvin North American Canoe Country, University of Minnesota Press, 2000, pp. 132–139.

206. For a fascinating tale on the sensitivity of the smolt stage in salmon development, see 'Maintenance of Angling through Smolt Releases in the Ranga River in Southern Iceland', by Throstur Ellidason et al. in International Council for the Exploration of the Sea: Council Meeting 1996 ANACAT Committee CM 1996/M:6.

207. Longfellow, Henry Wadsworth The Song of Hiawatha, Everyman, edited by Daniel Aaron.

208. For anyone keen to learn more about the way of the canoe, Bill Mason's seminal books Path of the Paddle and Song of the Paddle are unparalleled. Both have been published by Key Porter Books, Toronto. Bill Mason also produced a series of videos that accompany the technical coaching in Path of the Paddle, and I highly recommend these to anyone keen to improve their flatwater and whitewater paddling techniques.

209. Hayes, Derek First Crossing: Alexander Mackenzie, His Expedition Across North America, and the Opening of the Continent, Douglas & McIntyre, Vancouver/Toronto, 2001.

210. Lao Tzu Tao Te Ching, translated by Stanley Lombardo, Hackett Publishing Company Inc., 1993, Verse 8.

211. Rogers, Carl A. On Becoming a Person: A Therapist's View of Psychotherapy, Constable, London, 1961, p. 27.

212. LaChapelle, Dolores Deep Powder Snow: 40 Years of Ecstatic Skiing, Avalanches and Earth Wisdom, Kivaki Press, Durango, Colorado, 1993, pp. 45–46.

NOTES

213. Vycinas, Vincent Search for Gods, Martinus Nijhoff, The Hague, 1972, p. 177. Sourced from LaChapelle, Dolores Deep Powder Snow: 40 Years of Ecstatic Skiing, Avalanches and Earth Wisdom, Kivaki Press, Durango, Colorado, 1993, p. 67.

214. Olson, Sigurd The Singing Wilderness, University of Minnesota Press, 1956, p. 80. Reprinted with kind permission of Robert K. Olson.

215. Stonehouse as translated by Red Pine (Bill Porter) in The Zen Works of Stonehouse: Poems and Talks of a Fourteenth Century Chinese Hermit, Mercury House, San Francisco, 1999, p. 89. Reprinted with kind permission of Red Pine.

216. Henderson, Thomas The Findhorn: The River of Beauty, Grant & Murray, Edinburgh, 1932, p. 106.

217. White, Kenneth Open World: Collected Poems 1960–2000, Polygon, Edinburgh. Reproduced with kind permission of both the poet, Kenneth White, and Polygon (Birlinn Limited).

218. Fox, Warwick Toward a Transpersonal Ecology: Developing New Foundations for Environmentalism, State University of New York, 1995, p. 249.

219. Fox, Warwick Toward a Transpersonal Ecology: Developing New Foundations for Environmentalism, State University of New York, 1995, p. 252.

220. Hesse, Hermann Siddhartha, Picador 1998/Peter Owen Ltd, 1954, p. 116.

221. Thoreau, Henry David Cape Cod, Penguin, reprinted 1987, pp. 219–220.

222. The Kalevala: Epic of the Finnish People, translated by Eino Friberg. Otava Publishing Company Ltd, Helsinki, Finland, 1988, Runo 2, lines 225–232.